D0371094

Advance Praise for *The Treasure Hunt of Your Life*

If you're seeking answers to deep questions of identity, meaning, and purpose and wondering how to align your answers with the reality of today's world, this book will provide practical and inspiring advice for your journey. If it's time in your life to reflect and make informed choices, here's the guide for you.

—Carolyn Foster, M.A., career coach and founder, Creative Choices

Rebecca Schlatter unearths a great gift for readers by weaving her experience in ministry with her experience as a person, providing markers for those who are looking for guidance. This book inspires faith for our own journeys of vocation discernment: discovering who God has created, and is creating, us to be.

—The Rev. Greg Schaefer, Episcopal Lutheran Campus Ministry at Stanford University and author of *We Are the Young, Our Lives Are a Mystery: Pastoral Care with Generation X*

Companionship along the journey is exactly what this book offers. Like spiritual direction, this book will guide you to a purposeful attentiveness to God in every moment which leads to the abundant life God hopes for all of us.

—Sarah Cozzi, spiritual director and founder, Celebrate Living

This is a very special book, at once deeply personal and exceptionally insightful, informed not only by the wisdom of experience but also by the intelligence of a theologically-informed faith. Easily accessible, each page reflects the journey of an experienced pastor and theologian, a woman of faith who has learned much from her own searching, struggling and suffering, and who invites the reader to do the same. This book will help many people to discern their own vocation and discover a God who calls forth from us very human passions.

—Paul G. Crowley, S.J., Professor of Religious Studies, Santa Clara University and author of *Unwanted Wisdom: Suffering, the Cross and Hope*

THE TREASURE HUNT OF YOUR LIFE

To Dan —

God's blessings as you follow
the Spirit's leading

Rebecca Schlatter

The Treasure Hunt of Your Life

~

Seeking Your Calling,
Encountering God,
Finding Yourself

Rebecca Schlatter

REDWOOD VISIONS PRESS
2009

ISBN 978-0-615-31302-3

Unless otherwise noted, Scripture quotations are from the New Revised Standard Version of the Bible, copyright© 1989 by the Division of Christian Education of the National Council of Churches of Christ in the United States of America and are used by permission. All rights reserved.

Scripture quotations marked (NIV) are taken from the HOLY BIBLE, NEW INTERNATIONAL VERSION®. NIV®. Copyright© 1973, 1978, 1984 by International Bible Society. Used by permission of Zondervan. All rights reserved.

Redwood Visions Press
P.O. Box 6163
Reno, NV 89513-6163
www.rebeccaschlatter.com

Cover photograph by Mary Frances Errigo-Loggans

Designed by Robert Blesse

For Ingrid Nelson, 1973–2003

And for all who offer
good company

On your journey, may you …

Be what you want
Want what you need
Need what you learn
Learn what you find
Find what you seek
Seek what you imagine
Imagine what you know
Know what you say
Say what you see
See what you hold
Hold what you love
Love what you are.

Contents

Invitation: Finding Your Passion

"One day I was digging in the sand at the beach. I found something. It was a key! I dug some more. I found a treasure chest! It was locked so I opened it."

THAT'S THE ENTIRETY OF A STORY I wrote in first grade. By the time I rediscovered it twenty years later, I had just started seminary studies and was struggling with relationships, career, identity. I was confused and unsure, and my childhood story amazed me with its confidence— which, apparently, I had once possessed. At one time I had known that's how the world works: No matter where you are, you can bet there's a treasure around somewhere. If you find a key, you know the treasure is near. Once you find the treasure, your key will open it. Of course it will! The world is full of treasure just waiting to be sought and found.

But at twenty-six, I was no longer certain of anything. Yes, I was barreling down the road toward my "calling"— which was ordained ministry, as far as I could tell. Yet I was no closer to figuring out relationships or finances and not at all sure what my life would be like. In a paper that first year of seminary, I wrote, "A good part of the journey is figuring out what kind of journey it is." So far, my own journey has led through college, multiple faith communities and one live-in "intentional community," seminary, time off from seminary, and now three different "calls" (positions) in ministry. Sometimes I have been intentionally digging to see what I could find. Other times, exhausted by the search, I have felt more like I'm lost and begging to be found—by God, the universe, a significant other, *someone*. I spent much of college feeling lost, but at least I began to sense what I was seeking: I wanted to have a good life, whatever that meant. I felt alone with such questions, surrounded instead by conversations about having a good time or making a good living.

After college I stayed on the East Coast for a few years, far from my West Coast family. When I was twenty-two, I found myself walking the streets of Harvard Square at Christmastime. It was evening, and a soft snow was falling against the lighted shop windows. It felt like the set of a holiday movie, but my life seemed far from a happy ending. In fact, I was desperately lonely. I had not developed many close friendships in the months I had lived in Cambridge. My closest connections in town were the family whose children I took care of—my employers. Being with a family just seemed to prove how alone I was. I did not feel part of a family, nor was I in the love relationship for which I longed. My graduate studies in religion were a source of more confusion than comfort. I ached with longing as I walked through the snow to the bus stop, desperately wanting to know that I would not always feel so lonely and confused.

Invited to search

If I had met Jesus face to face in Harvard Square that night, perhaps he would have assured me that there was a treasure around there somewhere. Or he might have asked me the same thing he asks in the opening chapter of John's gospel, his first spoken words in that gospel: "What are you looking for?" I couldn't have answered that question back then, and neither could John the Baptist and two of John's disciples. They respond, "Rabbi, where are you staying?" Who can say exactly *what* we're looking for or what the treasure might turn out to be—a good life, our calling, our true selves, companionship, God? John's question is as good a response as any: I don't know what I'm looking for, but maybe you can show me where to find it.

Typical of a God who is both hidden and revealed, Jesus rarely answered such questions directly. Instead, he stirred people's imaginations with stories. In Matthew's gospel, one "treasure" is the kingdom of heaven.

The kingdom of heaven is like treasure hidden in a field, which someone found and hid; then in his joy he goes and sells all that he has and buys that field.

Again, the kingdom of heaven is like a merchant in search of fine pearls; on finding one pearl of great value, he went and sold all that he had and bought it (Matt.13:44–46).

We're left not knowing exactly what it *is*, but we know what it's *like*: something of great value, worth everything. And we never know where we'll find it—whether we'll stumble upon it or spend our lives searching for it.

In my recent ministries, I have worked with many young adults who are searching in one way or another. They want to see how their lives will "turn out." It's a yearning often shared by their parents and teachers and pastors, though the questions may be phrased differently. The young adults usually want to know all the things I wanted to know about my future: Will I be lonely? Will I be happy? Will I be safe and secure? Will my life have meaning and purpose and beauty? Will anyone's life be better because of me? These deep questions do not "turn out" with a single answer but continue to shape the questioner for a lifetime. Closer to the surface, the questions include:

- how they will make a living
- whether and how they will form a family of their own making
- how they will be connected with their family of origin
- what their career will be
- where they will make their home
- who will be their community
- whether their plans will bear fruit.

They want to know what to do—not only what practical decisions to make but what to do with their longings. They want to know how to find their passion and what to do with it. Many are looking for "communities of discernment": safe places where they can test ideas, commiserate on confusion, and celebrate moments of clarity.

Invited to discernment

For several years, I had the privilege of helping to form such communities of discernment on the campus of Santa Clara University. As Campus Minister for Vocation Discernment, it was my job to lead retreats in which students could get away from campus and deepen their understanding of their "vocation"—that is, their calling in life. (Most of us have multiple vocations, and the term goes way beyond simply "career," as we'll see later.) Some students simply wanted to be told what to do: "Just give me the right answer." But most students had already found plenty of people willing to give them answers: parents who wanted them to be secure, advisers and teachers and coaches who wanted them to be successful, peers who wanted them to be cool, spiritual leaders who wanted them to be virtuous and selfless. What they needed even more than answers was a way to sort through all that well-meant advice. They needed a way of sorting that took into account their own deepest longings and God's call, which were difficult to perceive in all that noise.

Practices of discernment—taught by religions for centuries—provide such ways of sorting. "Discernment" comes from a word meaning to separate or to sift. In contrast to "decision making," *discernment* implies an element of mystery. It involves listening along with acting. Paying attention to deeper movements of the heart and soul along with listing pros and cons. Prayer and meditation along with rational strategy. Being as well as doing. Discernment happens at the intersection of identity, faith, and action, where "who I am" meets "what I do" and where "talking the talk" becomes "walking the walk." Discernment means sorting out the core of your beliefs and convictions and noticing how your actions and relationships form the person you are becoming. For me, discernment has come to mean something even bigger than "making faithful decisions." It means that there is a treasure around here somewhere, waiting to be discovered.

As I spoke about discernment with students, I began to realize that I was also talking about different moments on my own journey: the twenty-two-year-old who longed to know how her life would turn out. The nineteen-year-old who longed for a community in which her gifts and talents would be received and her voice heard. The seventeen-year-old who was trying to find words for questions that seemed impossible to ask but too important not to ask. Too often along the journey, I had felt like I was alone in asking them. At thirty, I was still asking those questions about vocation and community in my marriage and ministry, but at least I had found some communities of discernment along the way.

Invited to stories

I had come to Santa Clara University with a mission: to provide students with company so that they might not have to feel as alone as I had. The "company" often took the form of stories; students appreciated stories of how life was "turning out" for us staff and faculty a little further on the journey. In fact, for the students who embraced vocation discernment, they wanted stories even more than they wanted practical information. They wanted to be inspired, not just educated. They didn't want to be "taught" discernment as much as they wanted to see it in action and try it themselves on their decisions about friendships, boyfriends and girlfriends, courses of study, study abroad, work, graduate studies, and their families of origin.

Discerning vocation is an art more than it is a science. No one really has a handle on how it works. It is both predictable and unpredictable, like any true experience of God. It is a mystery, and so we do with vocation what we are charged to do with mystery: hold it gently. Stand before it humbly, knowing that each story of vocation is unique. Stand before it daringly, knowing that all those stories belong to the same story of God's playful work in the world. Describe the mystery in metaphors which are true and rich and multilayered and which "fund the imagination."[1]

This book was born from those metaphors and stories and from the story behind my faith: the story of God acting in the world through the Spirit of Jesus. This goes beyond asking, "What would Jesus do?" That question might be helpful up to a point, but it does not go far enough to tell us what Jesus wants *us* to do in situations Jesus never faced. And it doesn't tell us *who* Jesus is asking us to become—which takes into account that we, in fact, are *not* Jesus. A much better question for discernment is, "What is Jesus doing?"

New Testament stories give us many examples of the way Jesus usually does things—the way he calls people to follow him, the way he comes to bring abundant life and love, the way he is present in difficult situations, the way he gives second chances and more, and the way he breathes new life into dead-end journeys. These are the kinds of things that Jesus usually did and still does through his Holy Spirit. Those stories of Jesus, read in tandem with our own, can help us discern what Jesus might be doing in our own lives and what he might be inviting us to do. Even more importantly, they give us a glimpse of who Jesus is inviting us to become.

Christian faith is a story of incarnation, of God becoming real and present and "fleshed out" in human life. Discernment, too, must be incarnational: it is where "who God is" meets "who I am," the person God has created and redeemed me to be. An experiential approach to discernment seems fitting for such a faith; God does not work only in theory but in the practice of people's lives. It's an appropriate way to read the Bible, which some have said *also* "reads us" by shedding new light on our deepest longings and our own lives' unfolding. It's like the woman who meets Jesus at the well in John 4. Jesus, she said, "told me everything I have ever done." Jesus often reveals to us a different way to tell our own story and to see his work within our past, present, and future.

My own story, of course, is still being told. Since that night in Harvard Square, I have found some communities of faith, work, friendship, and family. Some of those relationships have lasted; others have not. But in some ways I am still the woman who stood in the snow longing for assurance that deep and lasting connection is possible, that solitude does not always result in loneliness, that beauty is accessible everywhere, and that I would not die from the ache of longing. I want to bend time somehow so I can give my twenty-two-year-old self a glimpse of how rich her life would become—and, in fact, already was. Jungian analyst Marion Woodman holds out that possibility: "If you travel far enough, one day you will recognize yourself coming down the road to meet yourself, and you will say, 'Yes!'"[2]

In sharing stories of discernment with students, I have often met myself on the road and had the chance to say "yes"—not only to myself but also to God's mysterious work in my life. It has also given me the privilege of seeing young adults learn to give their wholehearted "yes" to the treasure of their lives and to new skills for seeking and recognizing it. Providing "company" in discernment has also meant keeping *myself* company—and writing the book I needed as a young adult.

Invited to your life

The invitation to a journey of discernment comes in many ways. Sometimes we are invited by the sudden joy of finding a "key"—a place where we belong or a person who brings out the best in us. At least as often, we are invited by pain. There's the painful longing for something or someone we can't name. There's the pain of life not working, with no idea of how to fix it. There's the anxiety of future pain that could come from current choices.

Anxiety about choices was something my students and I had in common. Whether this anxiety lived on the surface or was deeply buried, it usually stemmed from the fear that if we made a wrong choice—accepted or passed up a job, moved to a new city or not, married or broke up with a particular person, became a parent or not, continued schooling or not, chose a field we loved or one that would provide more security, retired or kept working—if we chose wrongly, *we would not be okay*. We would live *un*happily ever after. We would be financially insecure, or worse. We would end up alone. The stakes were high.

I also shared with many of my students the anxious desire to "do things right."

"Rightness" is easier to measure in some things than in others. Just ask my dad, an engineer by training, who was puzzled by my homework in any humanities subject: "But how do you know when you have the right answer?" When my students try to find their calling in life, they want to do it right, and they want to *know* they're doing it right. If other people, like their parents and professors, *also* know they're doing it right, so much the better. But how do you know when you have the right answer? On our deathbed, will we know if we've stayed "on track" and be able to give our life a thumbs-up or thumbs-down in terms of happiness or success? And how on Earth do you measure those, anyway?

My colleagues and I, working on vocation discernment, discussed this with more than a passing interest. Perhaps it was because we wanted to do our own jobs "right" by equipping students to find their vocation. A few things I knew:

I knew I wanted students to "be happy"—that's what my parents always said to me, and I suspected my students' parents would say the same thing.

I knew that achieving fame and accumulating money and "having the most toys" do not usually result in happiness. The same is true for anything else that can actually be measured with numbers—whether it's the size of one's house or the length of one's marriage.

I knew that I wanted students to be able to live with integrity—ethically and helpfully, yes, but also joyfully. Plenty of people want to "help people" as their life's goal, but I wanted them to do that out of joy and gratitude rather than out of duty and guilt.

I knew that I wanted students to "be authentic"—to live the unique life they've been given rather than trying to live someone else's life.

These things I knew, and this one I learned quickly: that when students tried to put a "good life" into words, they often mentioned this word: passion. This concept provided helpful common ground between students' desires and the vocation discernment resources we offered.

From the perspective of a fellow traveler on the journey of discernment, that made perfect sense. Apparently, "passion" is how many people are invited to this treasure hunt—either by its presence or by a desire to experience it. Living with passion means living in full color instead of in black and white. It's like listening to favorite music at full volume instead of elevator music. Passion is a meal with lots of good spices instead of cafeteria food. Passion is inspiring; it "breathes into" everything we do. It may not define a good life, but it surely is part of one.

Invited to passionate vocation

Let's be honest: "Finding your passion" sounds a lot more exciting than "discerning your vocation." I believe that you can't discern your vocation very well without at least addressing your passion. But this makes some people very nervous, and rightfully so: passion can be dangerous. Under the guise of following passion, people may simply seek out money, prestige, or sex. So I have encountered some people who say that we should stop talking about passion entirely when we talk about vocation, because passion is so easily distorted. On the other hand, perhaps this means we should talk about passion *more*, not less—so we can better describe passion as a connection with God and life's beautiful depths. It's bigger than any one *expression* of passion—it's a "fire in the belly" that contains a holy love and longing.

There's another danger here, too: the hope for a "passionate life" may place a greater burden on young people already facing myriad pressures. By encouraging young people to find their unique and sometimes elusive passion, we may inadvertently add burdens to the anxieties of young adult life. There's already the pressure to achieve all those milestones of young adulthood: financial security, lifelong partnership, more psychological independence, and so on—and then we burden them with finding things that use their passion and are *meaningful* too?

I used to worry about this, but I don't anymore. What's the alternative? Should we pretend that choices don't matter to one's quality of life? Should we encourage young adults to find a lousy job they hate that means nothing to them or anyone else? Of course not. The real question is whether we can live the paradox that God is found in the mundane, the everyday, and in suffering—everything that seems the opposite of a typical "passion." It's a challenge to comprehend the difference between a deep joy connected to passion and the more readily available "surface" feelings of fun or happiness. Real passion is a burden almost by definition, as its root word is "suffering." Biblical prophets—now there were some passionate folks!—were said to be given a "burden." To be sure, passion is not always fun.

Seeking your calling is more than just doing "what you're good at" or "whatever you enjoy," though those can be important signs along the way. Your calling tends to be whatever you do no matter what you're doing. I think of my dad, who, in many years as a student, a chemical engineer, a parent, a part-time professor, and a friend—no matter what his "official" role—couldn't help being a teacher. Teaching may not have been his *job* in most of those roles, but it was an aspect of his vocation. He couldn't seem to help it, and he was good at it, effortlessly. Another way to say this: a vocation is whatever you can't *not* do.

A vocation is where you belong, and where you feel at home, but in ways you are challenged to grow. It is a role (or place or task) in which you are most yourself, most authentic. By those definitions, your calling is not a destination but a journey, and a rather circular one at that. You seek your calling by noticing when and where you are called. You use the times when you feel most like yourself to help you discover yourself. In the same way, passion describes not only *what* we are looking for but also *how* and *why* we seek. Passion often shows up—as it will throughout this book—in a sense of empowerment, in desire, imagination, joy, and inspiration. All can provide helpful guidance on the journey, and like all manifestations of passion, they have to be sorted out with care.

Invited to this book

I didn't grow up hearing much about passion in church; my Lutheran tradition doesn't use that language often in talking about "vocation." This book, however, draws on resources from multiple Christian traditions. You'll find here some other concepts that my Lutheran tradition communicates very well: grace, discipleship, and a certain way of allowing mystery to remain mysterious, especially in the way God keeps seeking us even before we ourselves begin to seek. A bit of New Age language sneaks in, too, thanks to some helpful books and concepts I picked up on my spiritual meanderings in college. More recently, I have been profoundly shaped by the Catholic community at Santa Clara University in the Jesuit tradition, so you'll find influences from Ignatian spirituality (named for Saint Ignatius of Loyola, founder of the Society of Jesus, which is the official name of the religious order known as the Jesuits). Ignatian spirituality gave me a new way to value images, imagination, and empowerment in the spiritual life and in reading Scripture. This spirituality has also contributed some practical methods of discernment to my life and to this book. Finally, an evangelical Christian language creeps in by way of students and other individuals, especially my internship congregation, who have impassioned my faith along the way. All these languages have been helpful to me along the way.

I'm not an expert on discernment; like most people, I have foundered plenty of times in work and relationships. Mostly, I have learned discernment simply because I seem to *need* it so often. Each of us has to make sense of many languages and resources as we live, heal from, understand, and tell our own unfolding story. The "clues" interspersed throughout this book can help you explore your own resources. Some of my favorite resources are listed at the end of each chapter for you to explore further.

Whatever twists and turns you experience, the journey is worth the effort, and the skills it teaches you will contribute much to a good life— good for you and good for others too. Whether you are just embarking on your journey of discernment or whether you are reflecting back on an already long and winding road, I promise you, there's a treasure around here somewhere.

Further exploration

On the blessings and risks of passion and a "full-color" life:

- Lois Lowry's novel, *The Giver*, is written for a teenage audience, but it's a thought-provoking read for anyone considering the connection between passion and choices (New York: Laurel-Leaf Books, 1993).
- The film *Pleasantville* has the tagline, "Nothing is as simple as black and white." When people discover the "color" that comes with passion, things get more complicated (New Line Cinema, 1998).
- Ronald Rolheiser begins his book, *The Holy Longing*, with a famous quote on passion, attributed to Plato: "We are fired into life with a madness that comes from the gods...." It's a helpful way to begin *The Search for a Christian Spirituality*, as his subtitle says (New York: Doubleday, 1999).
- Brian J. Mahan invites readers to explore the intersections and conflicts between "worldly" ambitions and a spiritual and moral life in *Forgetting Ourselves on Purpose: Vocation and the Ethics of Ambition* (San Francisco: Jossey-Bass, 2002).

On vocational reflection:

- Programs for the Theological Exploration of Vocation (PTEV), an initiative of Lilly Endowment Inc. from 2000 to 2007, has a wealth of resources listed on the website, www.ptev.org. The site also contains history on specific projects at Santa Clara University and other schools that received PTEV grants.
- *Callings: Finding and Following an Authentic Life,* by Gregg Levoy, contains a staggering wealth of examples, real-life stories, quotations, and information (New York: Three Rivers Press, 1997).

SEEKING YOUR CALLING

ONE

The Treasure Hunt

Seek and you will find.
—Jesus (Matt. 7:7, NIV)

I WENT ON MY FIRST TREASURE HUNT when I was three. For Christmas that year, my parents had gotten me a large doll that could not be easily wrapped. Not wanting to ruin the surprise, they decided to hide it. But they didn't just leave me to search the house at random. They gave me a clue—a diagram, since I couldn't read yet—which sent me to a particular place like one of the kitchen cupboards. Taped inside the cupboard door was the next clue, which sent me to the TV, where a clue sent me to the grandfather clock. Eventually the clues led me to the bathtub, where I found the present. It was so much fun for everyone that each Christmas thereafter meant a treasure hunt for me and eventually my younger sister too.

On Christmas mornings, I never knew exactly what I was searching for. There was only one thing I knew about the end of the treasure hunt: it would be a *gift*. My search was enlivened by passion, grounded in hope, and powered by curiosity and a sense of adventure.

The next step

It wasn't until I started encouraging others in their search for vocation that I realized the connection between treasure hunts and my own life. No wonder I had missed it before: treasure hunts were so much more *joyful* than the anxious burden of life choices I'd been carrying around. To see the search for one's calling as a treasure hunt highlights the good news that God does not just leave us to search at random, hoping we'll stumble upon something worthwhile. God does show us the way but in a way consistent with God's nature—sometimes hidden, sometimes revealed in glimpses. The glimpses provide clues for the *next* choice, the *next* fork in the road. The clues don't usually lead directly to the treasure, but they do lead to the next step. Discernment means learning to know a clue when we see one—learning to recognize God-given glimpses of the next choice.

The journey looks and feels much different from this perspective, when it's not all about making the *right* choices—having the right plan, or finding just the right match for your talents, or finding just the right city or partner or opportunity at the right time. What a relief! It's only about *one* choice: the next one. It means we only have to see *one* step ahead—even when we want to see the next five years' steps, along with circumstances and outcomes impossible to predict. It means we don't have to "see around corners" ourselves, as the saying goes, but we can trust God to see the whole journey.

The Bible is full of stories of wanderers, exiles, refugees, nomads, apostles, and missionaries. Most often, God does not reveal the way all at once. When God sends Abraham out to a new land in Genesis 12, Abraham does not receive a detailed map. Neither do the people I know who have had to find not just a new land but new homes, relationships, jobs, cities, careers, and communities.

When Jesus says, "Follow me," presumably he is not considering where the disciples plan to be in five years, how much money they need in order to retire, or what a personality test says about their talents. And when Paul gets the call to go spread the gospel, he's not told the final destination. Christians have this tradition of uncertain journeys, but we too easily forget that the search for our callings is similarly risky. Often we ask instead for maps, plans, and destinations that will make us "safe" or "happy."

But is "safety" or "happiness" really the goal of our life's treasure hunt? Is "fun" what Jesus has in mind when he says "Follow me"? If he isn't thinking about our plans, our finances, or our personality, what *is* he thinking about? Does God want us to be happy, or useful, or "a good person," or something else? Before we can answer that, we have to wrestle with the stories behind our choices and try to figure out where God comes into them—or doesn't.

> **Clue:** At the end of the film Indiana Jones and the Last Crusade, Indiana must pick out the Holy Grail from a room full of various chalices. "Choose wisely," the old monk says, since it will mean life or death for Indiana and others.[1] When have you felt that serious about a choice you were facing, or what do you imagine it feels like?

Caught between stories

Much of our fear and anxiety finds its source in one of two stories we tell ourselves, consciously or not. The first story says that our happiness and success rest entirely on ourselves and our choices. The second story says that our choices don't affect our lives much at all.

In the first story, whatever happens, we are wholly responsible. We are supposed to anticipate all consequences of our decisions and prepare for all contingencies. If we are unhappy, unsuccessful, lonely, or insecure, it is our own fault; we should have chosen better. This first story places an unbearable burden on human beings. We have such limited vision and tendency to weakness; we *never* get things "just right." If we ever get close, we promptly bury ourselves under the responsibility of keeping things that way.

The second story produces a different kind of anxiety. No matter what we do, we are subject to forces beyond our control—destiny, fate, God's predestined will, whatever. These stories can be subtle and can easily turn us into victims of our lives and circumstances. Some people who don't worry at all about their choices (though not all of them) may have this story playing in the background. I discovered I had created a story like this even from my Lutheran background steeped in God's grace. I heard "God loves you no matter what" and turned it into "you can't do this wrong," which became "there's no way to do it right, either." I turned it into a story that told me nothing I did mattered much at all.

Sometimes, we merge these two stories to create other burdens. For example, "I am entirely responsible (story #1) for determining God's unalterable will for me (story #2) and making choices accordingly." Or we flip back and forth between stories. For example, when I was working as a hospital chaplain intern one summer, I met a young woman struggling with an eating disorder. As she talked about her plans for recovery and the new life choices she would make after she left the hospital, she alternated between the two stories. One day, she would say something that sounded like story #1: "I am going to take charge of my life. I am going to turn my life around. No one can do this for me." The next day, she would resign herself to her existing path in story #2: "This thing has beaten me. I need lots of help. I can't change things myself." Both seemed to make sense at the time, but both were inadequate. Story #1 relied on her own willpower, which was clearly inadequate for the immense hurdle of her illness. Story #2 did not give her the hope and empowerment she would need to move forward. Neither black nor white was working for her. They don't work for discerning one's calling, either.

Neither story provides much space for the "abundant life" Jesus says he wants to give us (John 10:10). Neither story holds much potential for joy, hope, connection, and self-esteem in hard times: Either hard times are our own fault, or we can't do anything about them at all. Either we trust ourselves alone, or we entrust ourselves to our circumstances, even when that means feeling like a victim.

When we need a new story, the treasure hunt provides one that accesses the truth behind *each* of these stories: No one can do it for you, but you don't have to do it alone.

> Clue: "Someone once asked Albert Einstein which question, among all his inquiries into the mysteries of the universe, is the most important question to ask. His reply: 'Is the universe a friendly place or not?' "[2] How would you answer that?

Paying attention

On my Christmas treasure hunts, it was easy to know when I was on the right track because I'd find clues—little pieces of paper taped in strange places. But in seeking one's calling, discerning the potential clues takes close attention. Clues come from two sources: inside and outside ourselves. We pay attention to what's happening inside us: how we feel and what we think. We also pay attention to what's happening outside us, what the circumstances are and what people tell us.

This attentiveness is the "work" of our life's treasure hunt. Like so many things in the spiritual life, it sounds simple but is surprisingly difficult. Attention unites our minds and hearts with what God is doing. It asks us to focus on the present and to see daily activities, work, and encounters as the places where God will show up. In fact, sometimes God shows up particularly clearly in the difficult, the sorrowful, and the tragic—the same places where Jesus did.[3] So attention to clues does *not* ask us to ignore what is difficult or painful. One day we might even see those difficulties as part of the raw material from which God shapes us and our vocations.

There are many metaphors for vocation discernment and many ways to pay attention. Some clues are auditory some are visual, and others are just a feeling. The term "vocation" comes from the word meaning "to call," and we often think of God as a caller and people as listeners. But information doesn't come only through our ears—we also have to *look* closely and *notice* or *feel* what is happening around us and within us. If God is an Artist, perhaps a potter, we could see vocation discernment visually as the ongoing revelation of the bigger picture or the true shape of the vessel. We could even see our own imperfections and internal or external chaos as part of what makes each of us an amazing work of art.

Internal clues: Ignatius of Loyola

Ignatian spirituality calls attention to feelings as an important source of clues. As we attend to our own feelings, desires, and reactions to the world around us, we see signs of what God is doing in our lives and where

God is leading us. This was one of the first things I learned when I arrived at Santa Clara University and began developing discernment retreats. I followed the suggestion to shape them around "Three Key Questions," as articulated by the Rev. Michael Himes, a Jesuit theologian at Boston College: What gives me joy? Am I good at it? Who needs me to do it?[4]

The question of joy may come naturally to some people but certainly not to all of us. When I heard these three questions, "what gives me joy" made it clear I was in a tradition different from what I'd known before. In contrast to many people who say they are seeking "what I really want," I'd learned to distrust desire as a source of information. My tradition has emphasized the way God speaks *outside* us; thus internal clues always seemed suspect. For years I believed that whatever spoke *within* me must not be God and would likely be opposed to God. Ignatian spirituality opened a way to understand those desires as potentially coming *from* God. Like passion, desire could be distorted by self-centeredness into mere appetite for pleasure and reward. But desire is not *always* turned against God. In fact, our longings could even turn us *toward* God.

No matter what our background is, we have to come to grips with internal clues through joy and desire. Some students struggled mightily with the question of joy and often answered "What gives me joy?" with some vague variation of "It gives me joy to be useful." But a sense of "usefulness" is primarily an external clue, because it means usefulness *to someone else*. "Usefulness" only goes so far, so how were they going to recognize internal clues if they couldn't perceive or articulate what they enjoyed or desired? I was dismayed precisely because they sounded like me. Somehow, I had grown up thinking God preferred usefulness to joy. I longed for young adults to experience the "abundant life" that Jesus offers *without* the suspicion that they must be ignoring their "duty" if life feels good.

Ignatius and his spiritual descendants gave me a way to articulate the relationship between discernment and the whole range of human emotions, including joy. To Ignatius, God communicates with people through the "movements of the heart," which means that paying attention to the pattern of feelings over time is a key way to attend to God's guidance. God is always leading us toward more love and more life, Ignatius reasoned, so feelings of "consolation" were often a sign that God was pointing in the direction of whatever was triggering those feelings. Consolation includes joy—a real, deep, liberating joy, as distinguished from "fun" or "happiness" or "satisfaction" (an important distinction but sometimes difficult to identify). Ignatius encouraged people to attend to consolation and its opposite, desolation, at least once daily in an "examination of consciousness."

When we attend to internal clues, we pay attention to our internal responses to what is happening around us. We also use our imagination to pay attention to our responses to what *might* happen. Ignatius, for example, encouraged people to use their imaginations in "trying on" different decisions to see which ones led to feelings of consolation or to desolation. Sometimes the clearest "call" may be the ability or inability to imagine oneself in a particular place. I still remember a Good Friday worship service when I was twenty-one, listening to a bland sermon in an almost empty church. I vividly imagined myself standing up and giving a better one. Arrogant, perhaps, but that experience also helped get my divinity school application into the mail.

Used alone, of course, imagination can easily steer us wrong. But as one tool among many, it can be quite helpful. And as with desire, I didn't know I had permission to use it—or rather, to let *God* use my imagination in communicating with me. Imagination also helps read our own story in the story of the Bible. I hadn't always read the Bible as so intertwined with my own life; until encountering Ignatius, I had not known that even in my encounters with Scripture, God sometimes used my own imagination to tell me what I needed to know.

I've been relieved to discover other religious traditions that say God's Spirit or voice speaks and is present *within* us. They finally gave me permission to see internal clues like joy and desire as guidance on the discernment journey—not the *only* guidance, but crucial guidance nevertheless. In campus ministry circles, the description of vocation I've heard quoted most often is this one by Frederick Buechner: "The place God calls you to is the place where your deep gladness and the world's deep hunger meet."[5] Some people are better at acknowledging one or the other, but the treasure hunt both offers and requires both kinds of clues.

> *Clue:* We can find clues in our reactions to all kinds of stories, including Scripture stories.[6] Reading with imagination is a good place to start. You can enter into a story as a character, the writer, or its first audience—then imagine "your" thoughts and feelings. Try the senses: what does the scene look like? Smell like? Sound like? Then, see what happens to you through the story.

External clues: Luther

By balancing internal and external clues, the treasure hunt frees us from being captive *either* to our desires *or* to a sense of duty alone. The other two questions suggested above call our attention to external clues: "What am I good at? Who needs me to do it?" As a Lutheran, I had learned how to notice these clues that come from outside ourselves. Luther emphasized that God speaks to us through the Word (the Bible) or through "the Word made flesh" in community or the neighbor in need, who could be anyone we encounter. For my students and me, outside clues were often recognizable in information about our *gifts* (the talents, experiences, ideas, and labor we could offer) and the *needs* we observed or heard about. Outside clues often came from people's feedback and the circumstances and opportunities we noticed. We will explore these kinds of clues further in the next chapter.

A real-life search for treasure

The following story of a college senior is one example of how clues work in a vocational treasure hunt. Jake told me he'd been seeking in that same manner since junior high school.

In seventh grade, Jake's mother suggested that he start volunteering. That made sense to Jake, and not long after, an opportunity arose through his mom's connections to an assisted-living center for the elderly. Following this clue, he started volunteering there, helping with activities and eventually leading some of them. People told him he was doing a good job, and they let him know how much he was needed there. Those were outside clues that he was on the right track, but he also discerned an inside clue: the job "fit" him, he said, and he enjoyed the medical setting.

Following this clue, Jake entered high school thinking he might be a doctor. But a bad experience in his chemistry class turned him off to science. Following a different clue from his earlier volunteering experience led him to consider leadership, and he became involved in student government. He found that he enjoyed this role, and he followed up on opportunities that led to student government at the district level, and then the state.

As he approached the end of high school, Jake knew he wanted to go to college. Medicine was out, and he didn't want to be a politician. He made the best decision he could: he applied to Santa Clara University to major in business, figuring it was at least practical. And he committed to keep looking for clues, telling himself: "If I don't like it, I can always leave." He did like it, and he didn't leave.

But at the end of his sophomore year, two years into his business major, he couldn't imagine doing any of the business careers he saw available to him. For once, he felt literally clueless. Then, on a weekend trip, something clicked: he rediscovered his interest in medical school. He found his professors receptive to the idea, so there was an outside clue—there was still time to finish the prerequisites for medical school. He followed the clue, began taking science classes, and this time, they went well.

In his senior year he did an internship in a hospital, where he tried out different roles in medical fields, from administration to social work to clinical work. Trying those roles gave him more information, more potential clues. He found that he really enjoyed the social work aspect as well as the clinical. *That* he could imagine himself doing. Now he was getting the hang of treasure-hunting: he had learned that the path to the treasure was not always straight but even when he'd reached a dead end, a new clue would turn up. And that's what happened. Jake wasn't accepted to medical school, but he held onto that social work clue and the possibility that he might get a social work degree instead.

Other circumstances, however, were pressing: he needed money to pay his bills, and his girlfriend was in graduate school in another city. The opportunity arose for a job close to where his girlfriend was living. His current job in business requires skills he learned following earlier clues, and it allows him to follow other kinds of clues in his relationship and in supporting himself. (One's financial situation can be a helpful outside clue!) By picking up external clues while staying attentive to the internal ones, Jake is faithfully traveling the many twists and turns of his own treasure hunt. And he's living out the saying, "Nothing one has learned is ever a waste."

At many points along the way, Jake had multiple options. Every treasure hunt is different, with a narrower or wider range of options, depending largely on factors beyond our control. Economics, family situation, location, national and ethnic background, personality, and education can all expand or limit the choices available to us.

Considering this diversity—and often inequality—in society at large, I've heard the concern that, by inviting private-college students at Santa Clara to consider their life choices, we unfairly overlooked people of limited means or disabilities who may perceive fewer choices in work. However, the terms "vocation" and "life choices" encompass so much more than work decisions alone; they refer to a whole range of decisions large and small, including decisions about faith and community and identity. Without exception, in those areas every individual has choices available to them which require paying attention to clues. I am grateful for my Lutheran tradition, in which "vocation" can apply equally to anyone, regardless of life circumstances, means, or abilities.

On a need-to-know basis

The concept of a treasure hunt gives us a good way to think about choices and their effects on a journey unfolding one day at a time. As we'll see later in the book, it's also a useful way to talk about following Jesus as a disciple—a relationship in which we are most often on a need-to-know basis about the next step.

Even when the next step seems dicey or ridiculous, we are called to an "ethic of risk."[7] I think of Abraham, who was not only called to a new land but then told to sacrifice his treasured son Isaac—now *there's* an unwelcome surprise (see Genesis 22:1–18). He keeps taking just one step at a time—starting on the journey, bringing along supplies for the sacrifice—and waiting for God to reveal each next step, including the one that ultimately saves Isaac from the knife. Then there's Dietrich Bonhoeffer, a German Lutheran pastor whose discipleship during World War II led him to take part in a murder plot against Adolf Hitler—an unconventional "destination" for a Christian leader, to be sure. That was the path Bonhoeffer discerned, even though the risks there ultimately cost him his life.

Stories like these make us wonder: can God really be trusted with our direction and destination? Whatever happened to safe and happy? A treasure hunt gives a different slant on "success." Things that might be called "failure" in light of one's plan or financial success are simply more information to be gathered on our treasure hunt. But, our anxiety asks, can the clues (and our interpretations of them) really be trusted?

Clues can be tricky. All we can do is keep paying attention and following the trail. When we seem to get off track, chances are good that we'll learn a lot about something else on our detour—and whatever we learn there won't be wasted and could even come in handy later. A detour can also be good news in a process of elimination. We may fail at something we try, or simply fail to enjoy something we thought we'd love. That may not help our self-esteem in the short-term, but it can be incredibly helpful for sorting through our interests and finding our calling in the long term.

Fortunately, a good treasure hunt does not require us to be certain or confident all the time. Anne Lamott, in her book *Traveling Mercies*, pictures a series of "staggers" or "lurches" between "lily pads"[8]—a series of places we stay and learn before we stagger on to the next clue. As we will see, this treasure hunt does not even depend on us finding just the right clues or interpreting them correctly. If you're clueless, or not sure which way the clue is pointing, follow your best guess and try something. Whatever you try, even if it is just sitting still, do it with the confidence that more clues will be revealed. Describing a similar confidence, one of Luther's most famous sayings captures the way that God's grace is evident even—or especially—in the possibility of wrong turns. "Sin boldly," Luther said, "but believe in the grace of God more boldly still."[9] By this definition, a good discerner isn't one who gets it right the first time. A good discerner is one who is willing to sin boldly, fall face-first into the grace of God, and let the grace of God lead the way.

> **Clue:** It's easy to become paralyzed, unable to see or follow clues, when you're afraid to make the wrong choice. Is there a choice in which you've been "paralyzed," where Luther's quote, "Sin boldly," could help you move forward?

Seeking joyfully

An anxious search for just the right life is painful. In contrast, a treasure hunt overflows with grace and freedom. Look at all the things you *don't* have to know, such as who you are, who God is, how it will turn out, what the destination is, or how to get there. A treasure hunt is so much more freeing than a map or a destination. And since it's a lot closer to how God works—sometimes hidden, sometimes revealed—it's a lot more likely to lead us to the "treasure" of a good life—one that is good for ourselves, for others, for the world.

As I look back to the joy of Christmas mornings, I wonder what it would take for us to approach our own seeking with as much excitement and anticipation as I experienced then. Even when the search was frustrating (some of my dad's clues could be pretty obscure), there was the thrill of the challenge and the confident anticipation of finding treasure. With that confidence, any anxiety was quickly transformed into curiosity. On Christmas, I learned that I could trust the search for several reasons: 1) because my parents wouldn't let me wander too far off track, 2) because I trusted that it would end in a gift, and 3) because, despite its difficulties, I knew that overall the challenge would be fun.

Of course, the treasure hunts of our lives have much higher stakes than a Christmas present. They often hold much deeper pain than the brief frustration I experienced on Christmas. But pain isn't the only source of anxiety. Rather, anxiety can come from the absence of those three conditions. Perhaps we don't believe that God can be trusted, and that God is always available to get us back on track. Perhaps we are skeptical about the value or even the existence of what we are seeking. Perhaps we don't believe that it will be any fun at all.

Those are a few of the reasons it helps to find company on this treasure hunt. No one can do this treasure hunt for us. But none of us does it alone, either. The search works best in community.

Further exploration

On internal clues:

- *A Room with a View*, a classic novel by E. M. Forster, invites the reader to consider "the holiness of direct desire" (New York: Dover Publications, 1995), 168.
- Parker J. Palmer draws on Quaker traditions in *Let Your Life Speak: Listening for the Voice of Vocation* (San Francisco: Jossey-Bass, 2000). Seeing an "inner light" in each person makes one particularly attentive to internal clues.

On external clues:

- Douglas J. Schuurman writes from a Protestant context in *Vocation: Discerning Our Callings in Life* (Grand Rapids, MI: William B. Eerdmans Publishing Co., 2004). His chapters on "Vocation, Decisions, and the Moral Life" consider external clues more than internal ones; in contrast to Palmer, he notes, "Luther and Calvin, along with the bulk of Christian tradition, are far less confident in the self and its aspirations" (123).

On clues in general:

- *Unfolding: The Perpetual Science of Your Soul's Work*, by Julia Mossbridge, offers practical experiments in which to seek clues (Novato, CA: New World Library, 2002).
- The film *Gattaca* is a great story of persistence and desire, especially relevant to those times when a slippery clue asks us to temporarily ignore what might be a sign and persist in our original direction (Columbia Pictures, 1997).

On Ignatian spirituality and the examination of consciousness:

- In their book *Sleeping with Bread: Holding What Gives You Life*, Dennis Linn, Sheila Fabricant Linn, and Matthew Linn offer a short, simple, and practical guide to the "examen," as it is also called (Mahwah, NJ: Paulist Press, 1995).
- *Inner Compass: An Invitation to Ignatian Spirituality*, by Margaret Silf (Chicago: Loyola Press, 1990), encourages reflection on one's everyday life based on Ignatius' Spiritual Exercises.

TWO

Clues in Community

Teach your mouth to say that which you have in your heart.
—Abba Poemen[1]

A<small>T THEIR BEST</small>, the people we spend time with—our family, friends, teachers, mentors—are a crucial source of companionship and clues. Feedback on someone's gifts and talents, opportunities for work or service, observations about needs—those clues can *only* come through one's community. But a community can contribute other things, too, some far less helpful: anxiety, unsolicited advice, pessimism, attempts to control, plans set in stone. At its worst, community can be an obstacle and a temptation to get off track.

And yet, where else but in community (large or small, near or far, current or historical) will we find our joy reflected back to us so we can notice it ourselves? Where else can we find "trial runs" for our gifts and people to let us know we are good at something? Where else would we encounter the needs of the world (or at least a small part of the world) in a way that might call forth those gifts? And once we have noticed the clues, where else would we find the courage, resources, and support to follow them into our future?

For all these reasons and more, if we're committed to looking for clues on the journey, we're also blessedly stuck with community of one kind or another.

Who helps you sing your song?

An early Christian saying advises, "Teach your mouth to say that which you have in your heart." This is a great saying for finding one's passion, which is sometimes compared to singing one's own song. To bring who you are to something you're a part of means first bringing forth the best of "who you are"—your song. For example, in my particular vocation of ministry, "teaching my mouth to say that which I have in my heart" could mean honesty and vulnerability in preaching or in pastoral conversation. In other vocations, the metaphor would be different: for an engineer, "singing" could mean constructing the possibility she envisions; for a father, it could mean being his very best self with his child. In any vocation, we need someone to draw out the songs within ourselves. We look for people—colleagues, a community of friends, a mentor, a spouse, a congregation—who can bring out the best in us. We need help knowing what's in our own hearts, waiting to be drawn out and voiced, embodied, enacted, or created.

One of the Bible's best-known songs is the one sung by Mary soon after she has become pregnant with Jesus. Often called the Magnificat, it begins, "My soul magnifies the Lord, and my spirit rejoices in God my Savior" (Luke 1:46–47). Mary's song has been read and sung by Christians throughout the ages but seldom with the recognition that, as Luke tells the story, she didn't bring forth her song alone. Mary's relative, Elizabeth, was pregnant at the same time. The Magnificat breaks forth during or immediately after Mary's visit to Elizabeth, whose pregnancy was also God-given and similarly "impossible." The angel had told Mary, "And now, your relative Elizabeth in her old age has also conceived a son; and this is the sixth month for her who was said to be barren. For nothing will be impossible with God" (vv. 36–37). Luke offers a wonderful image of these two pregnant women greeting each other as Mary arrives at Elizabeth's home: "When Elizabeth heard Mary's greeting, the child leaped in her womb" (v. 41). The image reminds me of the Hindu greeting, "Namaste," which means "The spirit in me greets the spirit in you." I picture Mary and Elizabeth that way: "The potential growing in me greets the potential growing in you."

Elizabeth quickly progresses from greeting to blessing: "And (she) exclaimed with a loud cry: 'Blessed are you among women, and blessed is the fruit of your womb! ... And blessed is she who believed that there would be a fulfillment of what was spoken to her by the Lord!' " (vv. 42, 45). Then Mary's mouth opens, and what's in her heart bursts forth in song. I wonder: If Elizabeth had not been there to acknowledge and bless what was yet to be born, could Mary have sung her song? And I wonder, too, who does that for you? Who greets the potential in you before it is even born? Who enables you to break forth with the best of what's in your heart?

> *Clue:* The Bible has plenty of famous songs, including a whole book of them in the Psalms ("Songs"). Which one(s) would come closest to saying what's in your heart? If none does, try writing your own.

Listening for joy and passion

Discernment requires cultivating the skill of listening to God, to oneself, and to others. We aren't always good at all of them, but one kind of listening often leads to another. We can start with whatever comes easiest and go from there. For example, some of my students found they were better at listening to someone else than to themselves or to God. In a common listening exercise sometimes called "contemplative listening," participants would pair up and take turns being the speaker and the listener. The speaker was the only one allowed to make any noise; listeners could express their attention in bodily and facial ways, but not with questions, comments, or even sounds—no "uh huh" or "oh." Many found the exercise difficult in either role, but overall they found themselves to be much better listeners of others—nonjudgmental, open-minded, and attuned to possibility—than they were of themselves. Then they could practice giving themselves and God the same patience and generosity they were eager to give to another person.

Even the best listener cannot tell you what your joy is. But others may notice when you are joyful and echo that back to you. Of course, their input is just information; *you* get to decide if they're right. Or you might catch joy from another person, because passion is contagious. If you really want to find your passion, hang out with passionate people and ask them how and why they do what they do.

You can see contagious passion exemplified in the movie *The Legend of Bagger Vance*.[2] Former championship golfer Rannulph Junuh (played by Matt Damon) finds himself at a crossroads in life: he has "lost his swing." His caddy Bagger Vance (Will Smith) shows up out of nowhere to help him find his "authentic swing"—a metaphor similar to "singing one's own song." In the exhibition game that is the climax of the movie, Junuh plays against two other champions. In the first half, he plays terribly, until he's twelve strokes behind the other two players. At that turning point, his caddy's young assistant helps Junuh remember his former passion and reconnect with his intense love for the game.

On the next tee, Junuh asks Bagger for advice and receives an odd suggestion: to carefully watch his competitor, Bobby Jones. Checking out the skills of the competition might not seem to be particularly motivating. But Bagger really doesn't care if Junuh *wins*; he cares that he find his authentic swing. Along with Junuh, we watch Bobby Jones' smooth and powerful swing. The scene is beautifully filmed and acted, and Bobby Jones has the kind of golf swing that makes you believe you could do it yourself if only you watched him enough. I have never played a real game of golf in my life, but even for me, when Bobby Jones is looking out over the field and the music starts playing, it makes me believe I *could* golf.

In catching passion, it doesn't even matter what the particular passion is. That is, I can learn plenty about passion from golfers or musicians or engineers, even if my vocation does not include those things. In many people's vocational stories, certain themes and common principles emerge: risk, serendipity, endurance, joy, courage, and persistence through uncertainty. Those, too, are contagious: hearing how those principles work in others' stories tunes me in to my own story.

Contagious passion can be one gift of "shadowing" programs, in which one person spends a day on the job with someone else. But it doesn't have to happen in a program. Sometimes it can mean asking passionate people about their stories. Or, like Rannulph Junuh and Bobby Jones, it can mean simply appreciating people doing what they do best—and trusting that each of us has a passionate, beautiful, and creative "best" in us, too.

> *Clue:* How do you notice joy in yourself? How might others notice? What do you look like, sound like, or move like when you are joyful?

Hearing your song

Sometimes we have to be heard by others before we can hear ourselves, and that "contemplative listening"—like Elizabeth's, perhaps—is a great gift we can give to each other. But the other half of *listening* to a calling is, paradoxically, finding one's own voice and *speaking* with it. To seek one's calling is to seek a place where one can hear and be heard.

Sometimes recognizing the sound of that voice—yours!—is an important clue to your next step. In my first call to a church, I couldn't have recognized it without the help of community. I had gone into the interview with uncertainty about the potential match. Afterward a friend asked me how it went. He inquired what they had asked me and how I had answered. Listening to me talk about the interview, he commented, "When you talk about the interview, you sound like a pastor." I'm not sure how that was possible, but it sounded right, and I accepted the position. I didn't *feel* like a pastor—I felt more like an impostor *playing* at being a pastor. And technically I *wasn't* even a pastor yet. In the Lutheran church, individuals are not ordained until they have received a "call" from a congregation. We call it the "external call" that comes from the church. Internally, *you* may think God is calling you, the church says, but that call has to be confirmed by *other people* who think God is calling you to minister *with them*.

So now, here was a congregation that wanted me to be its pastor: There was the external call. The question was, who was going to answer? My friend seemed to hear an answer from the pastor emerging in me. The following months gave me confidence that I could, in fact, *become* that person whom he had heard beginning to find her voice.

Gifts and needs

The idea that we see ourselves more clearly than anyone else does is an illusion of individualism. We need other people to help us see what we're good at. It is a cliché to say that one learns about oneself through encountering others, but it's also very true. After college I entered the Lutheran Volunteer Corps, where I lived in community with six other women. Early in the year, one of my housemates experienced a death in her family. She showed her sadness in an openly expressive way, which was unfamiliar to me, and I was so uncomfortable that I abruptly left the room, feeling extremely guilty. The next day we talked for a long time about the death and what it meant to her and how she felt. I tried to apologize for leaving the day before, but she stopped me. "You connect with people through ideas, not feelings," she said. "I don't do it that way, but you can—you have that gift." My housemates gave me the precious gift of appreciating my own gifts and showing me how they were needed in community.

I've seen vocation materials for campus ministry that ask "What are you good at?" as a reality check. They mean: community will tell you if you're kidding yourself about being good at something. It also works the other way around, when we're convinced that our talents are nothing special. If it's something that comes to us effortlessly, it's especially difficult to see it as a gift ourselves. It's easy to focus on the gifts we *don't* have, and sometimes we need the members of our community to point out the ones we *do* have. Often, they do this indirectly, by telling us how much our gift is needed. Living in community invites us to offer what we have—to bring who we are to something we're a part of. So it makes sense that you have to be a part of something bigger than yourself in order to find your calling. This is the other half of Frederick Buechner's saying: "the world's greatest need" which receives our deep gladness. Gifts are given not for our own sake but for the sake of community, the world's needs. In the Bible, Paul writes, "To each is given the manifestation of the Spirit for the common good" (1 Corin. 12:7). That's one reason that, in Christian tradition, a community is needed to "confirm" the internal call by affirming the connection between a person's gifts and passions and the common good. Sometimes this is practiced in a formal way, as in the Lutheran system of waiting for an "external call" before ordination. Less formally, in any calling it's easier to hear your own voice when you're surrounded by a community who can hear it and receive your gifts joyfully and gratefully. At least, that's the ideal; we'll see later in the book what happens when it doesn't work.

> *Clue:* Couples sometimes have "their song," which reminds them who they are together. Could individuals also have particular songs that serve as important reminders? What is "your song"? Which songs are reminders for you?

A place to be heard

When community works well, some have said, people can "hear each other into speech."[3] At first this seems backward; how can you hear something before it is spoken? Yet, that's exactly what we do in "contemplative" listening: listen for something not yet said. We "listen between the lines" and give the other person a chance to bring "who they are" to the surface.

If we are to find our voice, we need a community to bring it out through challenging us. The communities that "bring out the best" in us are rarely the ones handing us everything on a silver platter. We do need support, but it doesn't help our vocation to be pampered in community. When we are supported *too* much, we learn that what we have to bring isn't needed. Perhaps this is why students often agreed to *lead* vocation retreats at Santa Clara University, but it was sometimes difficult to find those who would *attend*. The attendees thought we just wanted to hand them something, but the leaders knew their best would be required. Higher expectations communicate challenge—something worthy of sacrifice, something which will *require* one's best to get over the hurdles.

In college, I was fortunate to find such a community challenging me to learn new skills, become a leader, and try out my "voice." With Outreach, as the organization was called, I participated in conferences, serve-a-thons, weekly volunteering at schools and art programs, and protests. This was all new to me; community service was not as popular then as it would become a decade later. When I was connecting with peers and organizations in our efforts to make a difference, I felt strong. I felt hopeful. I felt useful. I felt like I belonged. In this community, I felt the kinds of things I wish I could have felt in church, which has been an important community throughout my life but not always one that challenged me.

In church, I learned that I was forgiven, that I was justified by grace. I learned that nothing *I* could do could please God, but fortunately God loved me no matter what I did. I heard about vocation, which hinted at what *God* would do in my life but said little about what *I* would do in my life. The good news that I didn't have to work so hard to please God with my actions became the bad news for me: what I did was totally insignificant. So if it didn't matter, then what was I supposed to do? I may be able to trust *God* with my life, but how could I know if I could trust *myself* with it?

Years later, I rediscovered the second chapter of Mark's gospel, which summed up both the gift I had been given in the church and the gift I had found in Outreach. In the story, people have heard of Jesus' healing power and have crowded around him in a house. A paralyzed man is brought to Jesus, lowered through the roof on a mat by four others. Jesus tells him, "Son, your sins are forgiven" (Mark 2:5). Then he heals the man's paralysis.

As for me, I felt as if I'd been brought to Jesus by the church, like the paralytic lowered through the roof. Jesus spoke words of grace: "Your sins are forgiven." Then, it was as if the church had carried me away again, still paralyzed. But in Mark, *after* that word of grace comes a word of power: "Stand up and take your mat and walk" (v. 9). *That's* what I had been waiting for and had found in Outreach: empowerment.

Luther, of course, might be interpreted as empowering, when he talks about what a Christian *does* with one's freedom, in response to God's grace. But this is not what I heard growing up. I heard grace, and it stuck with me. I'm grateful for that; I can't imagine being grounded any other way. But I'm also grateful that I found empowerment *somewhere*. For me, it was a key aspect of growing up in the church rather than leaving it completely as a young adult, since most traditional churches are set up for people to either *be* a child or *have* one.

I thought that once I became a church leader myself, I would find empowerment in the church and encouragement to "get up and walk." Instead, I found more of what was probably supposed to be grace. It seemed that everyone wanted to "support" me as a young, new pastor of thirty. The support extended to the young adults who visited on Sunday mornings, too. Church leaders would ask how they could support and help these young people. Sure, this was better than trying to get them on a church committee within the first ten minutes. But it also communicated that they were people who had little to contribute: the congregation didn't need them; *they* needed *us* for "support." For some visitors, no doubt, the support was attractive, especially if they were used to having everything provided for them. But it's hard to grow up when you're surrounded by people trying to parent you. I imagine how different it would feel to hear something like, "Finally! Our 'common good' needed someone with gifts like yours." Some of the most grace-filled experiences I've had happened when people helped me see how I could contribute, how my gifts were needed and appreciated—not because I needed to earn their love but because I was an adult member of the community.

A community of discernment

So how do you know when you need support or challenge? When do you need a community that needs you, and when do you need one that is willing to carry you and provide for you? Often, we don't know *what* kind of community we need until we've found it—or its opposite. One way to tell what you need is to pay attention to what you want to give to others. And one way to *receive* what you need is to *offer* it to others. It's a version of the old cliché: "to have a friend, you have to be one." To find a community who will help you discern, it helps to *become* part of someone else's community of discernment.

A community of discernment is a group of people who, intentionally or not, provide helpful companionship on the treasure hunt. It can be a ready-made community, like a workplace, a congregation, a school or class, a team, or a family. Or it can be a group of disparate individuals who don't exist as a group except in your mind and heart—your coach, a teacher or professor, your friend's mom who's a great listener, your old Sunday School teacher who keeps in touch. We tried to offer such community on campus, but I wonder if any *other* communities consider it their job to be a community of discernment. After all, not everyone attends college, much less a Jesuit Catholic one. Where does everyone *else* find communities of discernment which draw out their emerging selves? We join someone's community of discernment when we listen "between the lines." Good supervisors and mentors do this. So do good parents, or a spouse. Sometimes ministers do too—churches and faith communities can indeed be communities of discernment. But they often do a better job of helping someone discern a call to church ministry than, say, a call to law or carpentry or parenthood.

To become a community of discernment for someone else, pay attention to how you listen. When you're doing it well, what the discerner hears most clearly is his or her own voice or God's, not yours. To avoid becoming more noise that drowns out the person's voice, it helps if we don't label choices and outcomes—such as "radical" or "successful." It helps if we don't idolize happiness, or security, or success. It helps to offer people a chance to be of service and to try out their gifts, even if they might fail. It helps to offer people a chance to live out their joy, even if it doesn't fit into a planned category like "teaching" or "banking" or "traveling."

It can be hard to love ourselves well in times of upheaval—times when we feel like we should know the answers or have more energy for the search, or when we don't like the clues we're getting (such as "take this low-paying job") and prefer to ignore them. These things also make it hard to love *other* people in their times of upheaval. I've met plenty of parents who are frustrated with their young-adult sons' and daughters' decisions. This makes sense; you can't even "see around corners" on your own treasure hunt, much less on someone else's, so there's not much you can control.

But it is possible to be good company even for a difficult journey. As a pastor, I aspire to this on behalf of my church. I want us to help people develop skills to hear the internal call—skills for listening to God and their deepest desires, skills for naming their interests and joys and talents. I also want people to have opportunities to hear the external call—leadership and volunteer opportunities, internships, trips that immerse them in another culture—in ways that confirm or deny the internal call through the needs of the community and world.

There is one more thing a community can do which is less concrete but perhaps even more important. It can invite individuals to the journey, and it can give them hope and faith to keep going even when they are stuck or clueless. It can give them the persistence and courage to follow the clues even when they are difficult or confusing. A community can help calm anxiety when it offers grace balanced with empowerment. Community can support, challenge, and hear someone into speech. We'll know it's working because our songs will be in harmony for the common good—our great joys meeting the world's great needs together.

> **Clue:** The film *Dead Poet's Society*, with Robin Williams as an unconventional prep school English teacher who encourages his students to "be extraordinary," is a classic vocation discernment story and an effective parable of helpful and unhelpful communities of discernment.[4] But I wonder if some young adults need, instead, the permission to be *ordinary*. Which do you need?

Further exploration

On hearing your song:

*   *Healing the Purpose of Your Life*, by Dennis Linn, Sheila Fabricant Linn, and Matthew Linn, connects vocation discernment with Ignatian spiritual practices. The book begins with a beautiful story of a whole community listening for a newborn child's song, then singing the song back to the person at key points throughout life (Mahwah, NJ: Paulist Press, 1999).
*   Not everyone has a "song," but everyone's heart contains *something*. In the animated film, *Happy Feet*, young penguins seek their "heartsong"—except for one tone-deaf penguin who discovers his "heartsong" is actually a dance (Kingdom Feature Productions, 2006).

On mirrors for your gifts:

*   Many secular resources for making career choices and finding a job complement a spiritual approach; for example, many can help you notice your gifts and talents and match them to the world's needs (or, they might say, to the market's opportunities). Richard Bolles' classic *What Color Is Your Parachute?* suggests ways to inventory your "transferable skills"—your gifts which can apply to various jobs, roles, and situations (Berkeley, CA: Ten Speed Press, revised annually).
*   Other inventories of styles and strengths can be found online; the Myers-Briggs Type Indicator (www.myersbriggs.org) and Strong Interest Inventory (www.cpp.com/products/strong/index.aspx) are frequently used.

On contemplative listening:

*   Like Santa Clara University's discernment project, many PTEV programs supported small groups in which members could listen contemplatively to each other and themselves. For one of those

approaches, read about "spiritual companioning" at the College of Saint Benedict/Saint John's University in Minnesota, www.csbsju. edu/journey/

- In *A Hidden Wholeness: The Journey Toward an Undivided Life*, Parker J. Palmer explores the way listening and being heard shape individuals, communities, and vocation (San Francisco: Jossey-Bass, 2004).

THREE

Called by Name

The important thing is this: to be able at any moment
to sacrifice what we are for what we could become.
—Charles Du Bos[1]

E VEN IF WE ARE EMBRACED by people who support and empower us, seeking our calling can be painful. It can require sacrifices that hurt. It can cost us more than we were prepared to give. It can ask us to let go of things we intended to hold onto forever, not least of which is "our plans." The treasure hunt teaches us repeatedly that we can't idolize anything along the way: not communities, not clues, not treasures, and certainly not ourselves.

Clues with your name on them

When I think of being surrounded by clues, I think of P. D. Eastman's classic children's book, *Are You My Mother?*[2] A newly hatched baby bird, never having seen its mother, falls from the nest and wanders around asking various animals and machines, "Are you my mother?" Sometimes the treasure hunt can feel like that wandering: "Are *you* my clue? Are you *my* clue?"

Clues can be tricky, so we sort carefully through feelings, feedback, and circumstances. Sometimes it's tricky not because we are clueless but because we are surrounded by so many potential clues—things that call out for our attention, advertise one thing and another, or tell us what we "should" do. Once we start noticing clues, we start finding them everywhere. That's why you have to look for clues with your own name on them. It's one thing to *seek* your calling. It's even harder to seek *your* calling.

On Christmas mornings, treasure hunting became trickier when my little sister got older and started having a treasure hunt of her own. My dad put out two sets of clues, but our treasure hunts overlapped, and sometimes we discovered each other's clues before our own. My dad learned quickly to mark the clues clearly with our names on them. Otherwise, I might find one of my sister's clues and get off track for my own search. Even though her clues might be easier to solve, there was no way I could make *her* clues lead to *my* present.

On our life's journeys, we learn to follow *our* clues to *our* calling, not someone else's. There are lots of things which are really good to do, but not all of them are ours to do. It's easy to feel pressured by people telling us that we're good at something, or that we are needed, or that something runs in the family. Those can all be clues, but we need to remember that our calling is not always what we *should* love, or what we have been *told* that we love, or even what we *want* to love.

Because passion is so personal, finding your calling is a lot like finding a place in which *you* are most *you*. The greatest goal is becoming yourself, not someone else. There's an old Jewish story about a great rabbi named Rabbi Zusya. When I imagine him and his fellow rabbis talking about who they'd like to become, Moses is at the top of the list. And yet, he said, God had made him Zusya. He said, "When I die, God will not ask me, 'Why were you not Moses?' He will ask me, 'Why were you not Zusya?' "[3]

Indeed, why not? Why is it so hard to be ourselves sometimes? Why is it so tempting to follow someone else's clues? For many reasons, one of which is the confounding, circular nature of this treasure hunt. How can I "be myself" when I don't know yet who "myself" is? How on Earth do we find clues with our name on them before we are clear on our identity?

The Good Shepherd

After I left home, I soon discovered that it wasn't just me trying to figure out which clues had my name on them. There was something else calling my name—or rather, *Someone* else. As a freshman in college, I was anxious about the future in every way. The country had just gone to war with Iraq the first time, and lots of things I thought were true and trustworthy seemed to be unraveling. Everything in my world seemed uncertain. I wasn't sure where my own life was going; all I knew was that I felt a tremendous pressure to make it go *somewhere*. Returning to school after winter break, I was depressed and worried to hear that my peers were already thinking about summer jobs and internships—in January! As spring break approached, rumors started to circulate about students who had sent out dozens of resumes and landed prestigious, even paid internships. As for me, I had no idea what I should do, or wanted to do. And I was convinced that everyone except me knew exactly what to do.

One afternoon, totally paralyzed, I lay on my dorm bed and stared at the ceiling. The future seemed a great void, and so did I. Then I heard a voice I didn't recognize saying, "I have called you by name; you are mine." The voice didn't seem to come from my own mind—it was a mess in there with all those voices of "not smart enough, not good enough, not connected enough." The words sounded vaguely familiar—was that in the Bible somewhere? Wherever it came from, I was pretty sure that "you are mine" meant I belonged to God. "Called by name" meant I had an identity that wasn't based on what I found or chose that summer—or ever.

Eventually, I located the source in Isaiah 43. If I'd also paid attention all those years to John 10, I might have recognized who it was calling me by name: Jesus, the Good Shepherd, who "calls his own sheep by name and leads them out" (John 10:3b). I desperately needed a word of grace, and that word was enough to hold onto this alternative to "it's all up to me to make the right choice and succeed."

I experienced this as grace-filled, particularly because I'd disconnected from church so thoroughly when I moved across the country. I had always imagined the Good Shepherd gathering the sheep together in one place, like those pictures of Jesus with the shepherd's staff, surrounded by children. As for me, I'd left the sheep pen when I left home. But being led *out* on a journey was right there in John's gospel, and it felt much truer to my experience as a young adult. Much later, I realized that God had been with me all the time out there, and perhaps starting on this journey had even been God's idea in the first place. God didn't abandon me once I was on the path but sent the Good Shepherd ahead as a guide: "When he has brought out all his own, he goes ahead of them, and the sheep follow him because they know his voice" (John 10:4).

On the journey with the Good Shepherd, our task is to learn discernment—that is, to hear and follow Jesus' voice and to recognize one's own name. This is discipleship at its simplest and its most radical: following Jesus no matter what, no matter where. From a Christian perspective, we might see the heart of vocation as following Jesus in whatever you end up doing. Jesus is pretty clear about what that takes: everything. In order to follow, we discover that we have to let go of a lot. Perhaps that's what Jesus meant when he said we have to *lose* our life in order to find it.

> **Clue:** Everyone follows something, or *many* things. What things or people or trends are you tempted to follow? Which ones keep you on track with your treasure hunt, and which ones could lead you off track?

Let go of clues

Often on the journey we have to let go of something we treasure when it turns out to be a clue to the next thing rather than the final destination. Clues are easy to mistake for treasure. It's easy to confuse the means with the end—especially when we get tired of asking, "Are we there yet?" But how do we know when we've arrived if we don't even know what the destination is?

In my Christmas treasure hunts, many times I thought I had found the gift and arrived at the destination when I was actually still on the way. I've done that in life, too. This was particularly true in one of my earliest significant life choices: choosing what to do and where to go after high school. I used the best discernment tools I had at the time and went off to college totally worn out by the decision making and ready to rest at my destination. But within the first few days, I was asked about my plans for a major, internships, and study abroad; there was no break from discerning. A slow learner, I experienced the same dismay years later when I started seminary. I thought the major discernment was deciding to *go* to seminary. Once there, I discovered a whole array of choices about types and locations of ministry.

I hadn't yet heard the saying by Gracie Allen, "Never place a period where God has placed a comma."[4] I was looking for the period, the sign that I could stop searching forever because I had arrived. This is both the good news and the bad news: with the mysterious nature of what we are seeking—our callings, God, ourselves—the treasure hunt never ends in our lifetime. We'll see later in the book how treasures appear along the way, but we never "arrive" once and for all. Once on the journey, we never stop receiving clues. As another saying goes, "This too shall pass." But alas, good and settled times pass, too, even when we want to declare them the "treasure" and end the search.

When we are stuck or clueless or uncomfortable, it is *good* news that we have not "arrived." More clues will come. In those cases, commas can alleviate our anxiety somewhat, because we know the story isn't over. When I graduated from seminary and was seeking a call to a congregation, I received this helpful advice: "Remember that your first call will probably not be your *last* call." No matter how pleasant or awful it is, the journey won't end there.

Commas can also provide the freedom we need in order to stay faithful to the treasure hunt. I remember two college students who had fallen seriously in love in their senior year. Given their different post-graduation plans, they were in great anxiety. What if they made the wrong choice?

What if they broke up or strained the relationship with distance to pursue their own plans and forever regretted giving up the relationship? Or what if one or both gave up graduate school plans to be together and regretted the losses to their careers? As they were leaning toward moving together to the city where Maggie would enter graduate school, she feared that Brandon would be jeopardizing a future career for their relationship. If the relationship didn't work out, how could she live with having "caused" those losses for him? Maggie's fear made sense, but it was based on the impossible attempt to see around corners. They couldn't see the future of the relationship or the way either of their career plans would unfold. So I asked Maggie, even if the relationship doesn't work out, what if you are simply God's way of getting Brandon to this new city? What if the relationship turns out to be a clue, not the destination—can you live with that? That "comma" provided the freedom necessary for them to take the next risky step by arranging their graduate school plans around being together as much as possible—and seeing what the next clue would bring. It gave them hope that things would work out somehow, no matter what they chose. They could trust that their choices would reveal further choices if they kept paying attention.

It's natural to hope for periods, not commas. In countless relationships and jobs, I have mistaken a clue for the treasure. Anytime we use the term "the one"—this person is the one, this job is the one, this home is the one—we risk putting a period where God has placed a comma. Though we do sometimes stay with a clue for a long time or a lifetime, life has many ways of keeping us moving on the journey. Relationships break up, or they are transformed by children or by illness or by geographical moves. Jobs lose funding or are changed by market forces. Homes are "traded up" or lost through natural disaster or financial situations. This too shall pass.

When we do have a plan in mind, the unexpected doesn't always sound like good news. We want it the way we've decided would be best—*this* relationship, *that* home, *this* job. I knew lots of college students with plans; some had arrived at college having already chosen their major, their extracurricular activities, and their careers. This is not necessarily a bad thing, but what about clues? Plan or no plan, the unexpected will arise. What if you don't like the classes you think you're going to major in and you turn out to be better at something else? What if your roommate gets involved with a club that looks interesting to you too? What if you volunteer at a place that really needs someone just like you? What if your health or finances take an unexpected turn? The unexpected will not be deterred by the fact that you have a plan.

On the flip side, I also know some young adults who have no plan and little or no motivation to find one. I wonder if, for some, that paralysis might be a sign of despair over finding the "right" vocation and adult livelihood. Either way, it's best to think of our plans like clues, not as something set in stone. Even with a plan, all we have to do is keep taking the next step that reveals itself and accept that sometimes it will lead to a new plan.

> **Clue:** The story of Jacob wrestling with the angel in Genesis 32:22–30 is a great companion in times of uncertainty, anxiety, and cluelessness. See what happens when you use Jacob's words on a situation you're wrestling with: "I will not let you go, unless you bless me" (v. 26).

Let go of your self

Sometimes we decide that our journey *has* to go a certain way because we think that's the path in which we can "be ourselves." But sometimes, "being ourselves" is not the point. Jesus calls people to "deny themselves and take up their cross and follow me" (Mark 8:34). As a young woman trying to find an adult self, I found this invitation unappealing, and it contributed to my distance from the church. *Deny* the self I was working so hard to develop? I learned how this doctrine of self-denial and self-sacrifice had been used against women, enforcing sexism for centuries, and I wanted no part of it. Shouldn't God *want* me to have the strong self of an adult woman?

Like so many of my struggles in faith, this one carried a blessing— just like the one in the Genesis story of Jacob wrestling with the angel all night and finally receiving the angel's blessing at dawn. After years of wrestling, I learned that self-denial means I'm allowed to be wrong about the self I'm becoming and the path laid out before me. I don't have to know exactly who I am or what my name is. God is revealing my self to me over time in life's clues.

Thanks to one of those clues, I entered seminary almost in spite of myself. The self I intended to be did not encompass becoming a Lutheran pastor. God must have made a mistake in my call to ministry. But the self I thought I was developing *did* include theological education, so I decided to start seminary and see what happened next. As I began, I kept a secret escape route in mind: Clinical Pastoral Education. I just knew that CPE would get me off the hook for ministry once and for all. CPE was required for ministry preparation. It meant spending a summer interning as a hospital chaplain—including work with patients and hospital staff and small group work with a supervisor to process the experience. Largely because of that intense processing, seminarians' CPE stories often sounded like veterans' war stories.

Well before I signed up for CPE, I knew that although it was a good thing for someone else to do, my name wasn't going to be on this clue. Sick people scared me; hospitals intimidated me. I just knew that I would flunk out of CPE—thus disqualifying myself from ordained ministry. Then I could finally go back to *my* plan, once I had proven God wrong about my call to ministry. Surely *then* God would see that I should be doing something much more cerebral for a career. Words were so much more predictable than sick and hurting people.

One of my biggest CPE anxieties was the unpredictable overnight on-call duty. One night, a man arrived in the intensive care unit and was pronounced brain-dead. I was paged and asked to keep his elderly mother company while she sat by his side, attempting to come to terms with this sudden news. During those long dark hours, we exchanged small talk, prayed a little, and sat in silence a lot. All of a sudden, she asked me, "Do you like being a chaplain?" I took a deep breath. How would I answer honestly, after all those months and even years of anticipating CPE with fear and distaste?

But when I reached down deep inside, what emerged was "yes." "Yes," I answered, "I do like being a chaplain." Perhaps it was sleep deprivation talking, or perhaps it was God. Sure, I was still afraid most of the time, but I was also deeply honored that people would open their hearts and lives to me at their most vulnerable times. I would not have called chaplaincy "fun" any more than the patients and their families were having "fun." But yes, I found a joy in it that utterly surprised me.

It was a blessing to discover that I had been so wrong about my journey. The self I thought I was feared pain and ran away from it. That self was obsessed with the desire to "do ministry right" and with my own inadequacy in facing illness and death. The life God was revealing to me was so much bigger than that: compassionate, openhearted, offering companionship rather than solutions. In order to grow into *that* self, I had to deny the self I thought I was. Only then could I embrace the "yes" that emerged suddenly from my own depths in the middle of the night.

The drama that night in the ICU was not about me and my self but about a family's pain. To remember my own internal drama so well seems contrary to the very point I'm making about self-denial. But vocations are like that—God works on the person through the role. Often, that work has meant denying the plans I've made and the self *I* think I am so I can become the self *God* thinks I am.

> *Clue:* Jesus' saying about "losing one's life in order to find it" appears at least once in all four gospels, suggesting that it might be central to his message.[5] What are you most afraid to lose? What might you hope to gain?

The cost of discipleship

On this journey of discipleship, I am both attracted and repelled by the radical simplicity of Jesus saying, "Follow me." When I hold onto many things (relationships, activities, interests, tasks) in my idea of a "full" life, I am repelled by the apparent single-mindedness of following. I become suspicious of what will be sacrificed along the way because, while I accept the *idea* of sacrifice, I want to *choose* the particular sacrifices myself. On the other hand, when life feels too full and when I feel pulled in myriad directions, the simplicity of following sounds like such a relief. When one's journey means daily juggling of competing priorities—work, family, education, spirituality, health—doing just one thing can sound more appealing.

It's so easy to get lost in many things that to do one thing—even one thing as broad as "follow Jesus"—can sound impossible. In the gospel of Luke, Jesus confronts people on their attachments to many things: "Whoever comes to me and does not hate father and mother, wife and children, brothers and sisters, yes, and even life itself, cannot be my disciple" (Luke 14:26). In the midst of a struggle to fit more and more into twenty-four hours, this is a radical call. I understand Jesus to be saying: "It's not about balance. It's not about juggling. It's not even about better time management. It's about me." That's how much Jesus wants to be in relationship with people. He says that without "hating"—that is, turning away from those attachments, discipleship really doesn't work.

I've heard people try to explain away the radical nature of the journey: "Well, Jesus can't really mean that." After all, what kind of "family values" would that be? Does he *really* want us to give up all these many things? I think so. In contrast to the idea of putting God *first* in life with our many things crowding in right behind, Jesus challenges us to live with God as the *one* thing in our lives. In its original language, disciple means "learner." The stuff of daily life becomes our own personal school for life with God. I imagine what it would look like and feel like to really live that way:

Instead of relationships becoming simply one more thing to put on the schedule, they could be "the way God teaches us about love."

Instead of work being whatever you do so that you can have time off later, it could be "the place we use the gifts God gave us in the community God gave us."

Instead of church becoming yet another thing to fit into a busy weekend, it could be "the way we deepen our relationship with God and community."

Instead of being the time when we rest up for more work, leisure time could be "a time to breathe deeply and to appreciate the beauty and wonder of God's world."

What would it cost to live that way? When I was growing up, I remember hearing sermons about "the cost of discipleship," a term made famous by Dietrich Bonhoeffer.[6] Scriptures such as Luke 14 detail that cost, and the sacrifices entailed in following Jesus. I saw my own attraction and repulsion to that reflected by the students I knew. They weren't averse to the cost of vocation; in fact, they sought it out. They were seeking something that was important enough to devote their lives to, whether that was work to be done or a relationship. They wanted their choices to serve some purpose. They didn't necessarily want to be superheroes, but the *Spiderman* movies helped us talk about the cost of vocation. In the first two, Peter Parker struggles with the sacrifices that his Spiderman "vocation" requires: the relationship he desires and the dependable job he needs. Peter asks plaintively whether his "life of responsibility" means that he can't have what he wants. Students fear that their vocation will challenge a relationship or prohibit the lifestyle they want. For example, a call to anything that requires long devoted hours might ask them to sacrifice family or other interests. They have already seen many variations of sacrifice in adults they know; in fact, many of their parents have sacrificed a great deal for their university education. Students wonder, do they too have the fortitude to make such choices now or in the future? Will their sacrifices be chosen or imposed on them? Hearing about the hours required of medical residents or the debt of volunteers who enter year-of-service programs gives many students pause.

Paradoxically, the same demands also *draw* many students to those paths. There is something attractive and "grown-up" about vocations that ask something of us. They've learned that there's a connection between what something costs and what it is worth. Students have told me recently that they think being a Christian should require sacrifices—it's a sign of something worth doing. Students want high expectations to live up to. In theory, they're willing and even eager to pay the cost, but they want a guarantee that they won't be miserable while doing it. They are looking for something that will not just *require* sacrifices but *enable* them. They are listening for a call so engaging that what they give up will seem paltry in comparison to what they receive.

On the other hand, it's possible to anticipate too many sacrifices, assuming that life is a zero-sum game—whatever you receive, you'll have to give something else up. If that were true, then happiness in one area would require sacrifice in another, because people would only be "allowed" a finite amount of happiness. As a young adult newly on my own, a friend told me that between the three areas of relationship, home, and work, people only experience satisfaction in two at a time.[7] I wonder whether such a presupposition is behind some of our fears of sacrifice. Perhaps Peter Parker could give us a more hopeful perspective: in the end, he surrenders to his vocation and gets the relationship, too. I want to believe that this kind of abundance is possible in ways we don't expect when we're living in a zero-sum game. Our lives have far more room for happiness than Peter and I had feared when all we could see before us were the costs.

Of course, everything has costs—not just discipleship. In my freshman year paralysis, I was starting to understand the cost of *non*-discipleship for me. The cost of *not* following Jesus was that I had to figure it all out myself—successfully, happily, ever after. On the other hand, if I followed the clues single-mindedly and wholeheartedly, trusting that they were given by the Good Shepherd who promised "abundant life"— perhaps then all those things I hoped for in a full life would be gathered under the umbrella of the *one* thing. "Strive for (God's) kingdom," Jesus says, "and these things will be given to you as well" (Luke 12:31).

As a young adult, I wanted guarantees that even if I did have to give something up, it would not be anything central to my happiness. Instead, I heard about trusting in God. That went well beyond sacrifice to surrender. Surrender was what happened when you truly lived this "one thing;" it was total, and much scarier. When our sacrificing turns into surrendering, we put the costs as well as the rewards in Someone else's hands. But to *whom* are we surrendering and can we trust that this One really does want the best for us in joy and abundance? We find out on the journey of seeking our calling, where we encounter God within and behind the journey.

> **Clue:** If you listed what makes your life "full," what would you include? How can you tell when your life is empty, full enough, or too full?

Further exploration

On letting go:

When you're torn between excitement and worry about a new direction, it helps to remember that you're not the only one struggling with such things. These songs and poem can remind you that "letting go" in its myriad forms is a common human experience.

- "Love's Recovery," song by the Indigo Girls (*Indigo Girls*, Sony Music Entertainment, 1989).
- "Unwritten," song by Natasha Bedingfield (*Unwritten*, Sony BMG Music Entertainment [UK] Limited, 2004).
- "One Thing," song by Finger Eleven (*Finger Eleven*, Wind-Up Entertainment, 2003).
- "Zero Circle," poem by Rumi, version by Coleman Barks in *Ten Poems to Change Your Life*, by Roger Housden (New York: Harmony Books, 2001, 43).

On leaving the sheep pen:

- In *Leaving Church: A Memoir of Faith*, Barbara Brown Taylor is discerning her way out of her role as an Episcopal priest serving a congregation and into a different calling. As the title says, she leaves one role but "keeps faith" in a different way (New York: HarperOne, 2006).
- In her memoir, *Girl Meets God*, Lauren F. Winner tells the story of moving between a different kind of "sheep pen": her choice to become an Orthodox Jew and her subsequent conversion to Christianity—neither of which is a simple "leaving" or "arriving" (New York: Random House, 2008).

On surrender:

- *A Path with Heart: A Guide through the Perils and Promises of Spiritual Life*, by Jack Kornfield, contains practical methods, meditations, and practices from the author's Buddhist perspective. Particularly when I was at a distance from my native Christian "sheep pen," I found this book helpful for deepening any spiritual journey. The book is also a reminder that Christianity is not the only religion or spiritual path that practices "surrender" (New York: Bantam Books, 1993).

ENCOUNTERING GOD

FOUR

A Big Enough God

One doesn't discover new lands without consenting
to lose sight of the shore for a long time.

—André Gide[1]

THERE ARE TIMES ON THE JOURNEY when we find ourselves way outside the sheep pen, being asked to let go of more than we ever thought possible and without a clue in sight. In my third year of working with students on vocation discernment, I was getting the hang of leading retreats, guiding discernment, and teaching the principles of vocation. However, my own life seemed to be getting more and more off track. My marriage was headed for divorce. My ministry at Santa Clara University seemed to be approaching the end, spiritually and administratively. That meant I was also losing my university apartment. It was a painful time of multiple losses, and it was difficult to talk about with students. After all, what I was experiencing was precisely what students were hoping to *avoid* by coming on the retreats I led. I had never offered guarantees, but still—what kind of credibility could I really have if my own discernment had led me to this awful, dark place? I was looking carefully, but no clues seemed to point a way out; I was stuck. In the midst of pain, uncertainty, and unhappiness, it seemed that I was emphatically *not* on the right track.

Along with the pain, I was rather peeved with God. I had worked so hard at discernment—following the clues, making sacrifices, listening carefully to God's call. Clearly, I thought, a loving God would not have led me into a painful two-year marriage. I had reached similar dead ends before. Years earlier, I enthusiastically began a degree at Harvard Divinity School, but that path seemed to lead directly off a cliff after only a year, and I had left. Later, after finishing my degree at Pacific Lutheran Theological Seminary, my first call in ministry ended after only a year and half. I had chalked those up to faulty discernment on my part, but these quick realizations that a choice was a mistake seemed to be becoming a pattern. So which were they: God's mistakes or mine?

Behind the peevishness was the astonishing arrogance of denial: I thought if I made all the right choices and took the right steps, I could avoid pain and loss. Never mind that every human life contains pain and loss. Never mind that I belong to a faith that has a crucifixion at its center. No, I had planned to skip all that sorrow. I was going to be *so* good at the treasure hunt that I would skillfully navigate my way around pain.

In hindsight, I could see that my expectations for discernment were way out of line. Like most kinds of denial, they didn't work for long. Thankfully, I belong to a faith that also has a resurrection at its center. This meant that maybe pain and loss weren't the end of the story. Even as I let go of life as I knew it, perhaps there was indeed something or Someone to let go *into*.

Surrender

Surrendering to God doesn't come naturally to most of us; it's even harder than sacrifice, but ultimately even more life-giving. In various ways we learn to do everything *besides* letting go. In movies, for example, we learn that when things get tough, you just *hold on*, with your knuckles white and your jaw clenched. You hold on until the underdog pulls ahead from last place, until an extra burst of adrenaline kicks in, or until the mystery check arrives in the mail. You hold on until the eleventh-hour rescue or miracle cure.

Mark's gospel tells the story of a woman suffering from hemorrhages who has been holding on for a very long time. She has been to every doctor, spent her last penny, and things have only gotten worse. She doesn't have a name, but we could fill in the name of people we know who have come to the end of hope, when every kind of chemotherapy and experimental treatment has been tried and failed, or when the final mediation attempt hasn't succeeded, or when all the appeals in court have been exhausted. Or when you're just exhausted, period. You've tried everything you know to make things better, and you have nowhere else to turn.

When you come to your end, the world says *hold on.* The gospel says *let go*: you're in God's territory now. Of course, the whole treasure hunt takes place in God's territory, but that's easy to ignore when you're still tackling the issue on your own—finding the right doctor, saying the right thing to fix the relationship, deciding on the right direction. Eventually, when you come to the end of your ideas, that's when that phrase starts to make some sense: "Let go and let God."

I used to hate that phrase. I usually hold on a long, long time, before I can be persuaded to let go. I don't give up control—that one last idea to try—without kicking and screaming. But it has become a bit easier since a middle-school student from church gave me an image for it.

She described her experience with a zip line, the kind often found on ropes courses. From one end of a long cable strung high in the air and slanted slightly downhill, the rider grabs a line hanging down from the cable and takes off. The line zips down the cable, with no help and no control from the rider. So here she was, sitting in a flimsy little harness far above the ground, holding on for dear life. But it was a long ride, and her arms tired quickly. When she couldn't hold on anymore, she let go. And then she discovered that it wasn't her arms that were holding her up at all. The harness wouldn't let her go, even when she couldn't hold on. When I heard her story, I pictured her letting go and discovering that she could fly.

Letting go is not easy, nor is it always passive. To the woman in Mark's gospel, "Let go and let God" was active and personal. The hemorrhages made her ritually unclean, which meant she was supposed to stay distant from people, but she ventured into the crowd anyway. She was looking for Jesus and thinking, "If I but touch his clothes, I will be made well." She was in God's territory: after hope, there was Jesus. He could be touched.

The challenge for us, I think, is actually to see and know and trust how "let go and let God" becomes personal, when we don't just reach out and touch Jesus in a crowd. For me, letting go means wrestling with my own doubts: God, are you paying attention? If I stop everything that hasn't worked before, won't things get even worse? Can I really trust you?

When the woman touches Jesus' clothes, she is healed. Jesus knows it, even though he hadn't seen her coming. He turns to look for her, and he makes it clear that the anonymous healing wasn't enough for him; he really wants to know her. That's what discipleship is meant to be. It's not about holding on until Jesus meets our needs and makes things turn out the way we want, like Superman. It's about letting go *into* an ongoing relationship with Someone who really wants to hold on to us. When we practice "let go and let God," we learn that even when we have lost hope and can't hold on any longer, we are *always* held by the One who will never let us go. After hope, we may not be able to stand, but we discover we can fly.

> *Clue:* Mark 5:28 says of the hemorrhaging woman, "She thought, 'If I but touch his clothes, I will be made well.' " After all her failed efforts, it's remarkable that she can still hope. In what have you put such hope? Was it worth it?

Wrong turns

When my colleagues and I told our own stories of vocation to each other or students, stories of lost hope or wrong turns often surfaced. In contrast, the project at Santa Clara University seemed set up to help students made good vocational choices—to hold on to their passion no matter what and "stay on track," so to speak. Those of us further on the journey, however, rarely talked about how well we had stayed on track and made good choices along the way. Rather, we spoke of detours, dead ends, painful losses, dreams we had to let go—all the things we seemed to be helping students avoid. Might we in fact lead them astray in a different way if we helped them "do it right" and thus miss the important learning experiences of "doing it wrong"?

If we had learned so much from those detours, was it even possible to do the journey "wrong"? Theologically, that was even harder to argue, thanks to Bible passages which say that there's no way to separate ourselves from God, no matter how badly we choose and no matter what happens to us. Psalm 139, for example, says that no matter which way we turn, we can't get outside God:

> Where can I go from your Spirit?
> Where can I flee from your presence?
> If I go up to the heavens, you are there;
> if I make my bed in the depths, you are there.
> If I rise on the wings of the dawn,
> if I settle on the far side of the sea,
> even there your hand will guide me,
> your right hand will hold me fast (vv. 7-10, NIV).

No matter what happens to us, we cannot get outside God's love, in the words of Romans 8:38–39:

> Neither death, nor life, nor angels, nor rulers, nor things present, nor things to come, nor powers, nor height, nor depth, nor anything else in all creation, will be able to separate us from the love of God in Christ Jesus our Lord.

Just before that promise comes a verse that is often quoted by people in awful, dark places: "We know that all things work together for good for those who love God, who are called according to his purpose" (Rom. 8:28). Just because life isn't going well doesn't mean that God has abandoned us. We need a bigger view of our life. And we need a bigger view of God, too, one whose reach extends far beyond anywhere we could ever go on this journey.

> *Clue:* "The courage to be is rooted in the God who
> appears when God has disappeared in the anxi-
> ety of doubt."[2] In other words, when you seem
> to have gone beyond the reach of the God you
> know—the God who appears then is big enough.
> Where have you been or where could you go that
> you thought God could not reach?

Stuck in dead ends

Fear of traveling beyond God's reach is one kind of difficulty. Not getting anywhere at all is another, leading us to wonder if God has abandoned our journey altogether. On the treasure hunt, we sometimes find ourselves stuck without a clue, not knowing which way to turn. Even worse, sometimes there doesn't seem to be any way to go at all. It's not uncommon to get stuck between a rock and a hard place in relationships, finances, jobs, and such. In Quaker terms, it's called "way closing."[3] It doesn't feel good, but it can still be one way of discerning: by process of elimination. The process works best if we let go and let God reveal a way out.

I picture this with the help of an experience driving in Berkeley, where I attended seminary. The city is a great place to live but can be a challenging place to park. One day my car got stuck—not between a rock and hard place *per se* but between two other cars. I had run an errand downtown, and when I saw a perfect parallel spot open up, I squeezed my way into the too-small space. When I tried to leave, I couldn't get out. With six inches on either end of the car, and my tires only about an inch from the curb, I couldn't move. All I could do was go back and forth repeatedly.

In life I had felt stuck like that. Not only in big decisions but also in little ones, such as the ones in daily seminary life: Either I could neglect some of my studies and activities, maybe jeopardizing the options for my future ministry, or I could work so hard that I'd forget why I was doing all this in the first place. Frankly, neither way sounded good, and I didn't perceive a lot of options besides trying harder at balance. But "try harder" isn't a very helpful strategy when you're already holding on as hard as you can. You may rev your engine, but really you just keep going forward and backward.

In a famous story told by Matthew, Mark, and Luke, Jesus gets stuck between a rock and a hard place. In the story, his challengers try to trap him by asking whether it's lawful to pay taxes to the emperor. It's a yes or no question, to which both answers are wrong—blasphemy on one side, sedition on the other. So what does Jesus do? He doesn't keep driving forward and backward. He goes sideways. He finds a way between the two wrong answers. "Give to the emperor the things that are the emperor's, and to God the things that are God's" (Mark 12:17).

In "letting go and letting God" we find the freedom to stop driving back and forth. We can rest our engine, because where could we go where God wouldn't already be waiting there for us? Maybe we'll even find the freedom to go sideways; there are plenty of directions toward God besides forward and backward. Ultimately we can even find the freedom that I glimpsed on that day in Berkeley, when I walked away from my stuck car and took the bus home.

Stuck and clueless 101: practicing gratitude

Before we discover that freedom, before God is revealed on the far side of the sea, what do we do when we don't know what to do—when more "doing" just tires us out by revving our engine or spinning our wheels? We could try what our religious forebears and spiritual gurus everywhere suggest: practice gratitude and see what changes. Of course, "have an attitude of gratitude" is a cheery piece of advice that is most annoying precisely when it is most necessary. Not once has that advice made me *feel* grateful. In theory, I agree: as an approach to life, gratitude is useful, healthful, and biblical. In practice, though, I resent the idea that gratitude could magically create happiness, cheerfulness, or clarity. But as I've come to know gratitude a bit better during my own times of not knowing where to go or what to do, I've found that it creates five things even more useful, healthful, and biblical than a sunny cheerfulness.

Awareness of consolation. In our daily lives, God is always leading us toward more love and more abundant life. So, the particular loving and life-giving things that make us feel most grateful just might turn out to be clues. When Saint Ignatius taught his companions to examine their consciousness at the end of each day, gratitude was central to the practice of locating and naming "consolation."

Wisdom. To gain wisdom for our journey, we might try doing what wisdom does. In the Bible, that's gratitude. Proverbs 8 imagines Wisdom as a divine being who was present with God when the world was being created. Wisdom was filled with delight, it says, "rejoicing in his inhabited world and delighting in the human race" (v. 31). Sharing that delight through gratitude brings us closer to Wisdom ourselves.

Forgiveness. Gratitude helps us let go of the ways we've been wronged—the very things that might have brought us to the far side of the sea in the first place. Fred Luskin's study on forgiveness, *Forgive for Good*, points to gratitude as central to the process of forgiving.[4] It's hard to keep feeling like a victim when you can find things to be grateful for. When you no longer feel like a victim, it's hard to stay resentful—even, as Luskin demonstrates, when you've been truly victimized. And letting go of resentment makes it much easier to let go into God.

Peace and love. If you're stuck, you might as well feel good where you are. Gratitude feeds our soul and even changes our neurochemistry. It's like the story told about a grandfather who teaches his grandson, "In each person, there are two wolves, always fighting each other. One is the wolf of love and peace; the other is the wolf of fear and anger." "Grandfather," asks the boy, "which one will win?" The grandfather answers, "Whichever one I feed."[5] The story describes perfectly the effect of gratitude: it's a powerful way to feed the wolf of peace and love in ourselves.

Hope. When we can summon gratitude for the past and present, it shifts how we feel about the future. Shortly after my life started falling apart, I started wearing a small silver key around my neck. It reminded me of my short story from first grade, about finding a key and then a treasure at the beach. With that little girl's confidence, I could already be grateful for the treasure that was around there somewhere.

> *Clue:* Many years ago, I dreamed that there were scary ghosts in my house, but as long as I kept singing, they wouldn't bother me. "Keep singing" is a good mantra for scary or depressing situations. Indeed, many hymns and spiritual songs are intended for such times. But really, I've found that any kind of song, from sad to silly, works to keep the ghosts at bay. What works for you?

A big enough God

Like gratitude, discernment isn't just for good times. I find it curious that people sometimes assume faith is impossible in hard times. Actually, the Bible doesn't have much to say about *good* times, except in the past or future. There's much more about being faithful and hopeful in the midst of exile, death, temptation, persecution, disaster, grief, loss…

Like Christian faith itself, discernment was made for the dark times, when it particularly helps to surrender our idea of who God is and what God is or should be doing. In contrast to the arrogance with which I was living, there's humility in realizing we really have no idea what good God may be working through the pains and losses of our lives. I could say, for example, that the whole point of my divorce and short-term ministries was to bring me to this life-giving ministry in Reno, but I really don't know that. It's just more arrogance, because in fact, God may be working on something else even now, within or beyond my current situation.

Though I don't believe God causes pain, I do believe that God uses our pain and losses quite creatively. A God who is bigger than anything we choose or experience is a God who can hold all the pieces when our lives and selves fall apart. This really big God can hold together the fragments of our stories. For example, the book of Colossians proclaims, "In him (Christ) all things hold together" (1:17). I love this image of God, because this is the kind of creativity that runs through the women of my family. My grandmother was a quilter who made beautiful works of art out of scraps of everyday fabrics—a dress here, a tie there. My mother quilts as well, but even more extraordinary than that work has been the scrapbooks she kept of my childhood and my sister's. Long before "scrap-booking" became a verb, she took fragments of our lives and organized them in books, creating order out of chaos. As for me, I have not done much quilting or scrapbooking, but I do love collage—like my mother and grandmother, taking fragments and making something whole.

Sometimes I've used collage as an invitation for God to hold my fall-en-apart pieces together, too. When my path of theological education seemed to drop abruptly off a cliff after my first year in divinity school, I took time off to regroup. When I crossed the country and arrived at my parents' house in a kind of mourning, I immediately began making a huge collage of various images and poems. It was a visual way of paying attention to the "bits and pieces" of my life. It helped me make sense of an abrupt and confusing decision and to trust once again that God the Artist really was still working on the big picture. It was a concrete way of hoping that God's loving and mysterious arrangement of those scattered and broken pieces might one day be revealed to me in all its beauty.

When God goes to work creatively on our pains and losses and the frag-ments of our stories—including stuck places and dead ends and wrong turns—something beautiful happens. Our lives do not become perfect, but they become more whole in the One who holds all things together. This is what redemption means: that *nothing* is lost, that *anything* can be redeemed by the God who is bigger than any choice we could make or any loss we could experience, even the loss of life itself. "For the Son of Man came to seek out and to save the lost," Jesus says (Luke 19:10). He desperately wants to hold onto us, even when we want to hold on to something else—a goal, a relationship, or an idea of ourselves. This is the hope in discernment: to surrender our arrogance and our own ideas so we can be held, and held together, by the One who will never let us go.

The best part is, it works even if we don't trust it. How *could* we trust deeply until we've experienced it? I started working on this book before everything in my life fell apart. The writing didn't work very well because even I wasn't really convinced. Several years later, my life is still not perfect, but in glimpses of wholeness I no longer feel as if I veered off the vocational road into a swamp and totaled my self. In that awful, dark place, there was no way I could have seen this "resurrection" coming. I couldn't see my losses as setbacks in a journey much bigger than I am. Before we find a basis for trust in our *own* experience, our faith relies on others'. We could rely on Thomas Merton, who concludes one prayer like this:

> Therefore will I trust you always though I may seem to be lost and in the shadow of death. I will not fear, for you are ever with me, and you will never leave me to face my perils alone.[6]

Even before we have been through our own perils and come through the shadow of death, we depend on others' testimony that

- dreams, journeys, and selves can survive setbacks and losses
- hard times do not mean God has abandoned us
- way closing will eventually point to another way opening; sometimes this way will be neither backward nor forward but sideways
- even if you let go, God won't
- after death comes resurrection
- no choice you make, and nothing you could experience, could ever take you outside God's love.

Sometimes the best we can do is to let go and take the leap into faith, trusting the saying: "The call of God will never take us where the grace of God cannot keep us." That's when we find out what, or who, is holding on to us.

Do choices matter after all?

If God is working for our wholeness and working for good in anything we choose, any direction we take, we might question the value of discernment at all. If God uses wrong turns for our good, why bother discerning? If my colleagues and I learned so much from our wrong turns, why weren't we *encouraging* our students to do so as well? Was any choice, any vocation, just as good as another? Perhaps what we needed to surrender most were our judgments on whether a choice was right or wrong.

And yet—this is mysterious. Some choices do seem to lead toward or away from God. In the next chapter, we'll see that there are ways we can cooperate with God in the divine, creative work leading toward wholeness. But to participate through our choices, we have to get a better sense of what God *might* be up to. We do this always with a huge dose of humility but with some audacity mixed in that we could learn to see more and more as a big enough God sees—with vision as big as the universe and as long as eternity.

So, instead of trying so hard to get it right in order to avoid pain, we could practice thinking big enough. When we think too small, we fall into a common misconception: that looking out for ourselves leads to the best we can get out of life. When we think too small, we might refuse the journey entirely—perhaps believing that there is nothing to seek or despairing that anything could be found. Even then, God accompanies us to the far side of the sea and never stops reaching out, working toward wholeness.

> *Clue:* Certainly sin is possible when we think too big, in arrogance or grandiosity. But it is also possible when we think too small and deny that God is big enough. When have you "thought too small," and what were the results?

Further exploration

On a big enough God:

• *A Big-Enough God: A Feminist's Search for a Joyful Theology,* by Sara Maitland, is most likely where I first heard the term. It's a good title, and it's a good book, too (New York: Riverhead Books, 1995).

On letting go and trusting:

• A number of David Wilcox's songs have thoughtful lyrics relevant to discernment, but "Farthest Shore" is especially helpful in those times when you have to leave everything behind on shore and just dive in (*Big Horizon,* 1994, A & M Records).

On gratitude in hard times:

• Fred Luskin's valuable *Forgive for Good: A Proven Prescription for Health and Happiness* details ways to practice gratitude on the way to forgiveness—which includes forgiving your life for the way it's turning out (San Francisco: HarperSanFrancisco, 2002).

When things get tough and "keep singing" might help, it helps to have songs to which you can sing along. These are some of my favorites by Christian artists:
• "If I Stand," song by Rich Mullins (*Songs,* 1996, Reunion Records)
• "Praise You in This Storm," song by Casting Crowns (*Lifesong,* 2005, Reunion Records)
• "Stand in the Rain," song by Superchick (*Beauty from Pain 1.1,* 2006, Inpop Records)
• "Testify to Love," song by Avalon (*A Maze of Grace,* 1997, Sparrow Records)

FIVE

God of Possibility

For mortals it is impossible, but not for God.
—Jesus (Mark 10:27, NIV)

FEW PEOPLE I KNOW have grown up with a childhood understanding of God that is able to withstand the challenges of adulthood. Fortunately, the journey can be an excellent way to become acquainted with a more grown-up God who can. Even if God doesn't change, we and our understandings surely do. Along the way, God reveals different aspects of the divine than those we had experienced before.

When I encountered these different aspects, I was literally at the far side of the sea. For my final year in seminary, I had applied to do my yearlong internship overseas. I was sent to Hong Kong, where I worked in both a Cantonese-speaking Chinese church and a mission outreach to Filipina women who worked in Hong Kong as domestic helpers. The God I encountered there was much bigger than the way I had known God before, but in some ways this God was smaller too—small enough to be seen in a foreign landscape, in relationships lost *and* found in translation, and in a seemingly insignificant ministry. There's a theological language for this: the incarnation, in which the infinite, big enough God becomes small enough to be known. In Hong Kong, I came to know more deeply and immediately aspects of God I hadn't truly appreciated before: grace, abundance, and possibility.

Before I went to Hong Kong, I attended several weeks of orientation with other missionaries being sent overseas. One teaching stood out above all the others: In a foreign land, you end up ignorant, lost, and an outsider. So, when you don't know, you can ask. When you are lost, you can seek and be looked for. When you are on the outside, you can knock on the door. This is all great news because of Jesus' promise: "Ask, and it will be given you; search, and you will find; knock, and the door will be opened for you" (Luke 11:9). As foreigners, we would spend a lot of time asking, seeking, and knocking, and we would see how Christ was present in our receiving, our finding, and in opening doors. This was a far cry from the missionaries of past generations "bringing Christ to the heathen" in foreign lands. Instead, we could believe and act as if wherever we were going in mission, God had always been there and was still way out ahead of us on the journey—ready to be asked and sought, and ready to open doors.

Grace

The theology I had brought with me to Hong Kong was inadequate for the grace I encountered there. I so desperately wanted to *matter*, and I thought that meant my actions, choices, and accomplishments had to matter. That made my internship very difficult, because I felt so ineffective and insignificant. I kept trying to follow clues and *do* stuff, and I kept running into walls of language or culture. I felt so useless, and I blamed God for sending me to the far side of the sea literally and figuratively: "God, whatever you are doing here, couldn't you have done it *some other way*?"[1]

To make matters worse, emails from my colleagues in American congregations detailed all the ways they were being useful to their congregations. They weren't dealing with the same kinds of walls, and they were teaching confirmation classes, designing worship services, and organizing stewardship campaigns. I longed for my ministry in Hong Kong to make a difference in that way. Instead, I was hanging out with people, trying to navigate my perilous way through small talk in Cantonese. I was eating a lot of dim sum. I attended prayer meetings at my church and sat there studying body language and listening for key words while people discussed their concerns in Cantonese. Every time I suggested I might be useful in some area, I felt rebuffed. So how was I supposed to be an effective intern and serve them if they wouldn't let me *do* anything?

And yet, they seemed to love me, even though I wasn't earning it at all. Both congregations to which I was assigned clearly loved me before I ever arrived. I was puzzled and even bothered by this, because how could they love me when they hadn't met me yet? How did they know I was going to deserve their love? Aha—that's when I discovered that despite a lifetime of hearing "grace" preached in church, I really did believe, deep down, that love must always be earned. My year in Hong Kong taught me that people love me because they are loving, not because I particularly deserve it that day. *Finally,* I got it: the same is true of God who wants to love me, not just to teach or improve me. I didn't notice such a graceful community and gracious God until I felt so useless and insignificant—until I had to stop *doing* things for people and just *be* with them.

Abundance

With the theology I had brought with me, there was no way I could believe that "being" was enough. I felt like Philip in the gospel of John, who on two occasions points out to Jesus—to *Jesus!*—that whatever he is suggesting is not enough. The first time is just before Jesus feeds five thousand people with five loaves of bread and two fish.

> When he (Jesus) looked up and saw a large crowd coming toward him, Jesus said to Philip, "Where are we to buy bread for these people to eat?" He said this to test him, for he himself knew what he was going to do. Philip answered him, "Six months' wages would not buy enough bread for each of them to get a little" (John 6:5–7).

Philip, of course, was wrong: once Jesus had done his work, what they had *was* enough, with leftovers besides. But later, during Jesus' "Farewell

Discourse" to his disciples (just before he was arrested and crucified), Philip is still asking for more.

> Jesus said to him, "I am the way, and the truth, and the life. No one comes to the Father except through me. If you know me, you will know my Father also. From now on you do know him and have seen him." Philip said to him, "Lord, show us the Father, and we will be satisfied" (John 14:6–8).

Poor Philip! Of course, what Jesus had shown them was *already* enough to satisfy them. Jesus' answer to Philip says as much in verse 9: "Have I been with you all this time, Philip, and you still do not know me? Whoever has seen me has seen the Father. How can you say, 'Show us the Father'?" Jesus had loved his disciples beyond their imagining—fed them and washed their feet—and was drawing them into the very heart of God. His presence was enough, like the few pieces of bread had been enough—miraculously sufficient. It shouldn't have been, but it was. Philip, stuck in scarcity like so many of us, couldn't see that.

It was easy to approach my ministry in Hong Kong (or any ministry, or any vocation) from a place of scarcity. When I contemplated how much time I was spending simply trying to communicate and understand—seven weeks of full-time language training—it seemed a waste of time and energy. When, beyond this year, would I ever need to know Cantonese? And even during that year—with so many Hong Kong people having a working knowledge of English, was it even worth it? Why should I bother to spend these scarce resources, when I could have spent them on something more useful? Others in Hong Kong picked up on this dynamic; they knew the language of scarcity too. Puzzled, they would ask me why I was bothering to learn the language. "So that I can talk with you," I would answer. They still seemed puzzled but also very pleased. I began to wonder whether learning Cantonese *was* the ministry.

In the smallest way, perhaps it echoed God's desire to be in relationship with people, and God's willingness to "speak our language" as a human being to do so. Was the incarnation itself a "waste" of divine time and energy? "Wastefulness" was part of my vocabulary but not of God's. While in Hong Kong, I read Barbara Kingsolver's novel, *Prodigal Summer*,[2] and her portrait of abundance reminded me how that adjective is sometimes used of God: God's "prodigal" love. For example, interpretations of Luke's gospel story of the so-called "Prodigal Son"—the son who wastes his father's resources—sometimes point out that the parable would be better called "The Prodigal Father." After all, it is the father (and God) who showers abundant love on the one who supposedly does not deserve it, with no regard to "wastefulness."

So there I was again, face to face with God's grace. In God's abundance, God has enough to give to everyone; grace is not a zero-sum game where, if one gets more, another gets less. In my internship and on life's journey, I didn't have to compare myself to anyone else—not to my fellow eager interns back in the States, and not to my own improbable expectations of how I would spend my time and energy on internship. No measuring was necessary, because "from his fullness"—God's prodigal abundance—"we have all received, grace upon grace" (John 1:16).

> *Clue:* What in your life—past, present, or future—seems impossible?

Possibility

In ministry, as in most vocations, there are moments which make me ask, "How did I get here?!" Times when it seems that nothing about my journey would have predicted this impossible situation. There were many such moments in my internship year. Sometimes it was because I felt particularly out of control of the clues. (In my interview for an overseas internship, when asked about my desired location, I told them honestly, "I have never pictured myself going to Asia." So how did I get to Hong Kong?!) Other times it was because I didn't have, or didn't think I had, the gifts or the experience to meet the demands of a particular situation. Like Philip, I found myself protesting, "There won't be enough"—skill, or love, or energy.

In the spring, I was recruited by the Hong Kong Lutheran seminary's worship professor to lead a liturgical dance workshop at a conference she had organized. My only experience with any kind of dance—and I mean *any* kind, unless you count yoga—had been the liturgical dance course I had recently taken in seminary, just for fun. Dance in worship was not widely known in the Lutheran church in Hong Kong, so I anticipated a small group for the workshop. However, I had far underestimated their curiosity, and I found myself frantically redoing the choreography to accommodate the thirty people who showed up the first day—none of whom spoke English as their first language and many of whom didn't speak it at all. It already should have been impossible—I didn't have nearly enough skill and energy and language for such an task. But there was more: I was also on crutches with a broken foot. Yet there I was, teaching thirty Chinese people how to dance prayerfully in worship.

One day during the worship conference, I met an American couple touring the seminary. Engaging in the usual small talk, they asked me what I was doing in Hong Kong, and I explained that I was doing my seminary internship there. They inquired whether it was an English-speaking church, and I said no. "Oh, do you speak Chinese?" they asked. I explained that I had managed to learn a little, and they looked puzzled—how could that be enough? "Isn't that impossible?" they asked. What could I say? Yes, and—thanks to some miraculous sufficiency—no. Then they asked what I was doing there at the seminary that day. I looked down at my crutches and smiled. "Teaching dance," I said.

Despite everything, the dance for the closing worship turned out beautifully. The *only* explanation I can find is God, because I know that all I contributed was equivalent to a few loaves and fish. I love this about ministry, and I'm certain that other vocations have these moments too: We get thrown into impossible situations we're not prepared for, some-times not gifted for, and we are led straight into the grace of God. My

American missionary friend in Hong Kong had an appropriate name for this. One time when I was preparing for another impossible task with the usual insufficient resources, she laughed, "You're really jumping into the arms of Jesus on this one, aren't you?"[3] That's exactly what I was doing, over and over again: jumping into the arms of Jesus. That's what you do when there's simply no place else to go: you take a leap into the one who promises, "But for God all things are possible" (Matt. 19:26).

Later I realized how many times I had encountered this God of the impossible even before internship. For example, when I was considering going into ministry, I was explaining to a young pastor I knew that I was "not cut out to be a pastor." She laughed out loud: "What on Earth does *that* mean?!" I gravely explained how I was "too much" this and "not enough" that. She shook her head. "There are *so many* ways to do ministry," she told me. God is *full* of possibilities. Or, as my American internship supervisor used to say, "God's other name is Surprise." If you want to find God in your journey, look for surprises in your life. Sometimes, Surprise's other name is God.

God on the journey

The mission educators were right: God was there in Hong Kong way ahead of me, waiting for me to catch up and be surprised by God's grace, abundance, and possibility. God was everywhere there: it was "prodigal summer" all year round in the abundant foliage, the extreme winds and rain, the overflowing city population. The community showered love prodigally on me that year—I might have been a foreigner, but I was *their* foreigner. God was in our efforts to understand each other and in our communication, which had moments of miraculous sufficiency when we understood so much more than had been said. God was there in my discovery that the language of "usefulness" and "wastefulness" was mine, not God's. Yes, I was spending all my time talking with people, eating, and praying with people for healing of all sorts of ills. But it occurred to me one day while reading the gospels that it sounded a lot like how Jesus spent his time. That hadn't felt like enough to me. Apparently (there's that arrogance again!), I had been seeking a calling that was *more useful than Jesus*—rather than letting him be miraculously sufficient for the particular ministry he had called me to that year.

God was very close indeed that year. Of course, God had always been showing up throughout the journey, as clue-giver, treasure, and even as clues. I didn't always *live* as if that were true, but I had *known* it for a long time. When I was nine, I wrote a story called "Hummingbirds and Snail Trails." There in the backyard playhouse under the redwood tree, that story became my masterpiece on seeking. Given that the heroine of the story is a talking rabbit, it has been tempting over the years to dismiss the story as childish. But in its own clumsy way, the story suggests the various ways that God shows up in the treasure hunt of our lives. Soon after beginning ministry with college students, I realized that the message I wanted to share was remarkably similar to "Hummingbirds and Snail Trails."

The story begins with Sunny Bunny being told her fortune by Gypsy Groundhog: "You will discover something new and wonderful someday." The next morning, she awakes to find a note under her pillow: "There are many wonderful treasures in these woods that animals nor people have never discovered. Follow these treasures, and at Wise Old Owl's tree, you will find a wonderful surprise. So long, and good luck!" The note was just signed "XXXX XXX XXX," but it included a P.S.: "The surprise can be shared with many things."

So Sunny sets out toward Wise Old Owl's tree, and before long she sees the first treasure: "A BEAUTIFUL hummingbird was hovering there, sucking a flower. 'Oh,' she whispered, 'I'll never forget this treasure as long as I live.' " The hummingbird then leads the way to several more "treasures": an impressive redwood, the lacelike tracks made by a snail, and a patch of dandelions lifted on the breeze. The story ends like this:

> She (Sunny) ran the rest of the way to Wise Old Owl's tree.
> "Wise Old Owl! Wise Owl!" she cried. "This note said that
> I would find a—"

"I know," said Wise Old Owl, "I sent it."

"Y-you?"

"Yes."

"Then—then what's the surprise—the one that can be shared with many things?"

"You have already found it yourself."

Sunny stared at him. "Me? But I only found a humming-bird, a giant redwood, some 'snail lace,' and dandelion seeds."

"That WAS the surprise, and it CAN be shared with many things." But Sunny wasn't listening to that part. So the gypsy was right, she thought, this was my discovery.

"Oh, thank you, Wise Old Owl!" With those words Sunny ran home to tell her mama and her friends. Wise Old Owl smiled and said, "That is one smart bunny!" and the humming-bird nodded. The End.

Goodness, beauty, and truth are often "hiding" in plain view and re-quire attentiveness to notice them. That is what I learned again in Hong Kong, and what I wanted to share with students who were seeking their vocation. I didn't have language for this attentiveness until I discovered Saint Ignatius, but apparently I'd been practicing something like it since childhood.

In the story I wrote, Wise Old Owl is both the origin and the destina-tion of the journey. In the story I live, God plays precisely that role. Like Wise Old Owl, who sent the note, God first invites us to the journey. Receiving and answering the invitation is a way of knowing God. In col-lege I had a friend, an agnostic with a Christian upbringing, with whom I discussed spirituality endlessly. We agreed that out of all the images of God we had encountered, the one we liked best was Author: God as the author of our stories and of the world's story. When we finally turned in our senior theses, we went to a favorite hill to pour out libations of thanksgiving with soda from the Computer Center machine, a small to-ken of the vast amount of caffeine that had fueled our work. We toasted our various thanksgivings for the process, and our final "toast" was to "whatever it is that makes us do this." Here's to the One who enables us to celebrate, allows us to remember, inspires us, gives us our own stories to live, and invites us to seek.

Along the way, God gives wonderful clues—some are beautiful, others are heartbreaking, and many are humorous. ("Talking, eating, and praying?!" In Hong Kong, the joke was on me.) Then, because God has become incarnate in the world, when we see Christ in another and find direction there, we might say that God even *becomes* clues sometimes. In the hummingbird, I see something which is clearly in cahoots with the owl, leading Sunny right to his own tree. It sounds suspiciously like the Holy Spirit: one who accompanies us on the way and gets our attention, sometimes even flying around our heads with a holy impatience and leading us to know the infinite Creator God.

Wise Old Owl points to his own tree as the destination of the journey. But even at age nine, I was beginning to see that, as it is said, "It's the journey, not the destination, that matters." Life is not so much about where you end up as it is about what you learn to love along the way. Just as Sunny discovered, when we find beauty worth loving, it becomes the gift we have to give away.

> **Clue.** In *Let Your Life Speak*, Parker Palmer encourages looking for one's "birthright gifts," which may have been lost in the process of growing up.[4] It's a helpful way to think about *what* we seek when we seek our self and vocation. I've wondered whether my young poet-writer self is one of those birthright gifts found in the process of seeking my own vocation. What might yours be?

An ethic of the beautiful

Our entire journey is enfolded in God—the what, the why, and even the who of our seeking. As Luther taught, the Holy Spirit's work in us enables us to seek in the first place. God is also *how* we seek; as we become acquainted with this clue-giver, we get better at seeing and interpreting clues. When we see grace, abundance, and possibility, we should suspect that God is at work. Seeing God in this way has offered new questions for discernment, such as, "Is this the kind of thing that a graceful, prodigal, impossible God does?" "How am I being invited to notice something worth loving and to share that?"

In the context of Plato's ancient categories of the good, the true, and the beautiful, we can hear these questions calling our attention to the beautiful. Thus they sound slightly different from the questions we often ask based on "what is the good thing to do" or "what is true here." This shift makes integrity not only a moral question but an aesthetic one. It makes discernment an art more than a science. I have been an artist my whole life, trying to see and evoke the beautiful, but only recently have I come to see its ethical implications. In beauty, as in art, there is no such thing as insignificance—even absence has presence. In a blue painting, one tiny speck of white changes the whole effect.

One of my encounters with this kind of beauty came during my summer at a French boarding school when I was sixteen and found myself in a small, provincial town in the south of France, Le Chambon-sur-Lignon. The landscape and my experience there were beautiful, and when I returned to the States, I discovered that the town had a beautiful story as well. During World War II, that town of about five thousand people hid and saved about the same number of people (the majority of them Jews), thanks largely to that very school, which had opened at that time and which I had attended half a century later. Nothing I had noticed in the town openly told the story, and it was quite possible to spend six weeks there and never learn any of the story.[5] I heard it after I returned, through *Weapons of the Spirit*,[6] a film which had just been made by Pierre Sauvage, who had been born and protected in Le Chambon during the war.

The people of Le Chambon are also immortalized in a book by the ethicist Philip Hallie, *Lest Innocent Blood Be Shed*.[7] According to Hallie, in his research the Chambonnais repeatedly told him that they hadn't done anything heroic—they just did what needed to be done. They weren't necessarily trying to be *good*, and they were not proclaiming the *true* from the rooftops. But was it the kind of thing the graceful, abundant, impossible God of the beautiful would do? Absolutely. One thing that makes the story beautiful is the sheer insignificance of it. In the context of the Holocaust, five thousand people is not a terribly large number, nor is it obvious that the Chambonnais' "heroism" swayed any political outcome. Were the risk and time and energy worth it? Like God's abundant grace, surely they were not wasted.

An ethic of the true might look to history and ask "What has Jesus done?" An ethic of the good offers other questions to discernment, such as "What would Jesus do?" An ethic of the beautiful, however, leads us to ask, "What is Jesus doing?" What is Jesus doing in one's life and in the world? How can I be the kind of person and do the kinds of things that live *with* rather than *against* that beautiful, Spirit-inspired activity? Since I can never know for sure exactly what God is doing, I get to keep following to see where the journey goes next. Believing that God has the last word, I have a pretty good guess about where it ends—with God's eternal equivalent of Wise Old Owl's tree. But like any really good story, just because I know the ending doesn't mean I don't want to hear it. I'm *in* this story, and I know that what I do and who I am affects the story; there is no such thing as insignificance. Nothing is wasted—not clues, not love.

> **Clue:** Jesus is said to "intercede" for us through his Spirit, praying the prayers for which we have no words (Rom. 8:26–27, Heb. 7:25). What is Jesus' prayer for you right now? What are his greatest hopes for you?

What is Jesus doing?

Like Philip and all of Jesus' disciples, I am a *mathetes*, which is the Greek word used for "disciple" in the gospels. It literally means "learner." I rarely see clearly where Jesus is going, but I want to follow. Like Philip, I often can't see what Jesus is doing, and I fail to notice God showing up in my own journey or in others'. So Jesus' response to Philip is comforting to me, too. "Believe me that I am in the Father and the Father is in me; but if you do not, then believe me because of the works themselves" (John 14:11). In other words, Jesus says, if you can't yet believe this about the indwelling of me and the Father, then at least hang onto what you have heard and seen. Hang onto my words and deeds. Hang onto what I am about to do when I lay down my life for my friends. "Very truly, I tell you, the one who believes in me will also do the works that I do and, in fact, will do greater works than these, because I am going to the Father" (v. 12). Even after I go away, Jesus says, watch how those words and deeds and loving sacrifices will continue and even grow. You'll see me in words and deeds of beauty: healing and compassion, peace and forgiveness, and love that sacrifices for another. It will be enough.

So what is Jesus doing? He's doing the beautiful, risky, prodigally loving things he always does. Centuries of seekers and travelers have discovered that that is enough—enough to discern, love, teach, heal, and share far beyond our own human weakness and self-centeredness. In these works of the Spirit within and through us, generations have learned to recognize Jesus, because this is exactly how he promised long ago to dwell with us forever.

- "I am the vine," Jesus promised, showing up in clues of connection and true intimacy.
- "I am the good shepherd." When we are lost, there is Jesus coming to look for us.
- "I am the way." Whenever we find a way forward through impossibly hard times, that is Jesus.
- "I am the truth." In insight, clarity, and discernment, we can hear Jesus' voice.

- "I am the resurrection and the life." When we suffer impossible losses, Jesus shows up, eventually, in an inexplicable hope beyond all hope.
- "I am the bread of life." Jesus sustains us on our journeys by nourishing all kinds of hungers.

The Bible teaches that Jesus was God-become-flesh, God "incarnate." The promise is that he walks with and among and in us still, in all these ways. But if that's true, then why is it so difficult sometimes to have a clue about what God is doing and where the Spirit is leading?

'Functional atheism'

To fully answer that question would require a far greater understanding of God's mind and human weakness than I claim to have. But I do know that *believing* in Christ's active presence and *living as if* Christ is active are two different things. Instead of the latter, many of us live in what Parker Palmer calls "functional atheism," which is

> ... the belief that ultimate responsibility for everything rests with us. This is the unconscious, unexamined conviction that if anything decent is going to happen here, we are the ones who must make it happen—a conviction held even by people who talk a good game about God.[8]

I heard an example of this once on a retreat, when small groups were reflecting on where we see God most readily. Several members of our group mentioned seeing God in nature. I wondered aloud why we so often find it easier to see God's handiwork in a tree than in other people. After all, our faith says that both are created by God, and indeed Genesis tells us that God took *extra* care in creating human beings in God's own image. In response, as a good example of functional atheism, one theory proposed that trees were somehow a more "pure" creation of God and remained the way "God made them." People, on the other hand ... It was implied that we don't stay "the way God made us" but rather become something different when we somehow take over the job of our own creation. We moved on quickly in our discussion without further exploration, but the idea kept bothering me. It sounded like a theology in which God just powers up people like a wind-up toy and then leaves them to run by their own devices. In contrast, nothing in my theology or experience says that God somehow abandoned me after my creation: "Here's everything you'll need for your lifetime—good luck to you." And yet, even if we have that faith, sometimes we *live* as if everything is up to us. I know I have lived much of my life that way—as if my life and growth were my responsibilities alone, and my calling was a burden I had to find and carry out myself.

To find clues by asking "What is Jesus doing?" and to live by following them, one has to not only believe in the incarnation but also live as if it were true. Our faith and our life are not always so congruent, however. In fact, sometimes I think we keep them separate almost intentionally, a separation that is most clear in the Christian festival that celebrates the incarnation: Christmas.

The Christmas story easily becomes almost too precious to be real, practically enshrined, so that nothing can touch it and ruin it with real life. We guard it in something like a snow globe I found one year: Joseph and Mary and the manger in the globe above, with the Three Kings below. When you shook it, glitter gently fell onto the manger. It even played music, "O Holy Night." It was lovely, and completely untouchable by real life. It was protected from life's danger and messiness, up on a shelf. That's just how the incarnation can become: untouchable and completely disconnected from our real life. We often live our journeys that way—we are "down here" with our human burdens and chaos and struggles, and God is somewhere far away in a lovely heaven that has little everyday effect on us and our choices.

This is not the incarnation story the Bible tells. That one is *all about* real life. Life in the flesh is messy, yes, but God was not content to stay compartmentalized in the snow globe, distant from human life. And so

Jesus came to walk in our shoes—the real ones that aren't always glittering and attractive. Living as if the incarnation is true, however, is not about smashing the snow globe and demystifying the story, removing all the glitter and beauty from it. Instead, it's about *re*mystifying human life—noticing "treasures" like the ones Sunny Bunny discovered. When Jesus is out of the snow globe, walking around among us, it calls us to pay attention differently and to see the sacredness of our own lives. Jesus is among us, walking around in our shoes.

Saint Athanasius said, "The Son of God became human so that we might become divine."[9] Other theologians have echoed this as they talk about the incarnation's consequences for our lives. In other words, Jesus came to walk in our shoes: so what? Well, our lives do not become perfect, but they become more whole. When you get your shoes back, after Jesus has taken them out for a spin, there is often a greater sense of sacredness, perhaps a little glitter left behind. Life appears more peaceful, saner, more beautiful, even in the midst of trials and tribulations. Our lives become sacred, not only after death in some faraway heaven but even in the midst of real, everyday, messy life.

We often need someone else's help to see this. It can be very hard, when *we* don't want to be in our shoes, to imagine why *God* would want to be in our shoes. It's hard to imagine being loved so prodigally, so sometimes it's easier to see Jesus present in someone else's life than in one's own. When my life was falling apart, a friend of mine pointed out that light to me. She knew I was in pain, but alongside that pain she could also see things I couldn't, and she gently helped me see them too. What was Jesus doing? He was mourning the losses along with me and bringing a gradual healing along with the possibility of freedom. Her response to my litany of difficulties was oddly, divinely appropriate: "How cool!" She knew those difficulties could be signs of the presence of Jesus walking in our shoes and doing his ultimately beautiful work.

We are fortunate when we have such attentive communities of discernment. Many people turn to a "spiritual director" to provide such community—someone who can help them ask, "*Where is God* in this situation, thought or feeling, or decision?" To answer that, we have to re-member that Jesus doesn't just walk in our "church shoes." He walks in all kinds of shoes in all kinds of places—workplaces, homes, schools—and he especially loves hanging out with the poor and the sick and the lonely.

This active presence of Jesus can be a little too close for comfort some-times, especially when he is stirring up change in our lives, causing us to question, calling us to heal or to be of service. At those times it's tempt-ing to put Jesus back in the snow globe, compartmentalizing him right out of our messy, crazy, busy lives. We go back to our functional atheism and keep him up on the shelf, bringing him down just for prayer and meditation, religious activities, holidays, those glittering and beautiful times. Better to keep him out of our fears and failures and daily lives and choices. Then we can preserve the perfect idea of God intact, without letting real life ruin it. Well, we can try to put Jesus up on the shelf in the snow globe, but he just won't stay there. He will not even stay in church, safely compartmentalized and distant from real life. He breaks out into real life one way or another, continuing his risky and beautiful and prodi-gally loving work.

> *Clue:* It may be more important to *live* as if the incarnation is true than to *believe* in it intellectu-ally. Fortunately, it is much easier to change our actions than to change our beliefs. Once we *do* something differently, we might even discover we're *thinking* differently. How do you live as if God has become flesh and is present in your jour-ney? If you did live that way, what would change in your life?

Conversion

"Functional atheism" is what life looks like when one *doesn't* live as if Jesus is active and present. So what does it look like when one *does*? Answer-ing this question is like trying to prove the effectiveness of prayer: what kind of difference can be measured? Some of the answer surely would be in how it feels—more peaceful, more whole, more sane, more beautiful. People do tend to make better decisions when they are calm and not driven by fear, anxiety, or resentment. With more courage, freedom, and hope, I believe we make better choices and live a better life—better for ourselves and of better service to those around us. If part of the journey is figuring out what kind of journey it is, then perhaps one way to approach the difference is to look at the adjectives we would use for this journey. Adventurous or torturous? Joyful or frustrating? Patient or frantic? Gift or burden? Encountering the God of possibility changes the quality of the journey in the same way that reframing a question changes the answer you get. When we reframe "Am I on the right track?" as "What is Jesus doing?" we can stop looking for our own rightness and attend to beauty instead—which is a much more compassionate and joyful way to live.

However, often life does *not* feel serene or make sense, and it doesn't mean that God has abandoned us or that we're necessarily on the wrong track. This is where theology gives way to testimony. Here is mine: at some point after encountering the God of possibility, and *knowing* that's who I had encountered, I began to believe, most of the time, that there was enough. Enough love, enough time, enough energy, enough gifts for my vocations, enough grace to go around. I was converted to the God of possibility.

That conversion turned me around in the midst of my journey, similar to what happens when one reaches the center of a labyrinth.[10] Christians have patterned spiritual journeying on labyrinths for centuries. This conversion forms the center of the labyrinth that is this book. Since then, I have traveled back over much the same ground, which is why the second half of the book seems to mirror the first. However, with more attention to grace, abundance, possibility, and the beauty of what Jesus might be doing, I started traveling my journey with a changed heart and mind, new eyes and ears.

In God's abundant grace, I started paying much more attention to who God was forming me to *be* through my experiences, choices, and learnings, rather than worrying so much about what I should *do*. That, in turn, helped me see my vocations as gifts to be lived into, not as burdens to lug around. Before that encounter, I wasn't entirely sure that "I have called you by name; you are mine" was really *good* news. But when the God of possibility calls me by name, I know there is joy and adventure on the way, and a grace big enough to cover the risks and messiness that are on the way, too.

The word "conversion" is almost too big and important for this turning. I am not actually all that different than I was. As a Lutheran, I learned much more about gradual rather than sudden change, and this conversion, too, was gradual. It reminds me of some artwork that a seminary classmate made for an assignment in our class studying Paul's writing. He folded a piece of paper as an accordion and on every other panel, he drew a scene representing the "old creation"—black and white scarcity, decay, and absence. On the other pieces he drew the "new creation"—colorful, abundant life and presence. When it was standing up as an accordion, if you looked at it from one angle, all you could see was old creation. Just a few steps to the side, however, the new creation was right there.[11]

That's how my conversion has been—just a few steps away from where I was but a very different view. Honestly, I can't say that I *always* believe in God's beauty and abundance, nor do I always journey as if I do. But I have started believing it more often. It's not much, I know. In fact, the difference is about the size of a tiny mustard seed. But even this can be enough for miracles to happen; Jesus said, "If you have faith the size of a mustard seed, you will say to this mountain, 'Move from here to there,' and it will move; and nothing will be impossible for you" (Matt. 17:20).

> *Clue:* To discover what kind of journey you're on, it can be helpful to draw a "life map": a timeline (linear or not) on which you mark significant events or periods and their effect on you (highs, lows, epiphanies, and so on). Try a life map on which you list adjectives to describe your journey at different times.

Further exploration

On possibility:

- *The Art of Possibility,* by Rosamund Stone Zander and Benjamin Zander, is fun to read but hard to describe. Here's how it begins: "Unlike the genre of how-to books that offer strategies to surmount the hurdles of a competitive world and move out ahead, the objective of this book is to provide the reader the means to lift off from that world of struggle and sail into a vast universe of possibility" (New York: Penguin Books, 2000), 1.
- During my internship, I first learned Don Moen's song, "God Will Make a Way," in its Chinese translation. It worked for my "impossible" internship, and it works for other impossible situations, too (*God Will Make a Way: The Best of Don Moen,* Integrity Media, Inc., 2003).

On incarnation:

- *Encounters with Silence,* a devotional-style book by Karl Rahner, S.J., discusses God becoming "small enough" so as not to overwhelm people (trans. James M. Denske, S.J.; Westminster, MD: The Newman Press, 1960), 11–17.
- "The Call," George Herbert's seventeenth-century poem, is perhaps better known by its first line, "Come my Way, my Truth, my Life." It was set to music by Ralph Vaughan Williams (*Five Mystical Songs,* 1911) in a hymn known by either title. I fell in love with the hymn while in Hong Kong, and it remains one of my favorite portrayals of incarnation and new creation. You can find the words and Williams' tune at www.cyberhymnal.org.

On the history of Le Chambon-sur-Lignon, France:

- *Lest Innocent Blood Be Shed: The Story of the Village of Le Chambon and How Goodness Happened There,* by Philip Hallie, remains the definitive history of the town during the Second World War (New York: Harper & Row, 1979).

- The film *Weapons of the Spirit* (Pierre Sauvage Productions, 1989) and other information can be found on the Chambon Foundation's website, www.chambon.org.

SIX

Big Enough Grace

Almighty God, who has given you the will to do these things,
graciously give you the strength and compassion to perform them.
— Prayer said at ordinations and
installations in the Lutheran church[1]

As WE BEGIN to see ourselves as God might, with compassion and also
with clarity, we quickly come face to face with our brokenness and
weakness. Then we have to come to terms with journeying with, or in
spite of, that weakness. Behind the question "Am I on the right track?"
lives another: "Am I strong enough for this journey?"

In Hong Kong, I discovered God revealed in new ways, but my own
brokenness was revealed as well. The journey had taken me to the far side
of the sea in more ways than one; I had never felt so alone and off-track
as I felt on many days that year. The journey seemed to require more
strength, skill, and patience than I would ever have. In the final months
of my internship, I was also *literally* not "up to" any journey because of
a broken foot encased in a toe-to-knee cast. I couldn't walk on that leg,
making any travel treacherous, especially because of frequent summer
rain, which kept the sidewalks near my home slick with moss. Never
mind "leaving the shore"—I couldn't even leave my house.

And yet, at the same time, I was learning to live with a God of possibility. *Without* that big enough God, indeed we can't be enough for all the
journey asks of us. But what does the journey look like *with* this God?

> **Clue:** Sometimes difficult situations or cluelessness cause us to question our journeying ability. Paradoxically, grace and abundance can also cause us to question—as Peter does in Luke 5:8, when he responds to his abundant, Jesus-inspired catch of fish by falling at Jesus' feet, saying: "Go away from me, Lord, for I am a sinful man!" What circumstances have caused you to question your ability to journey?

Faith as a crutch

I walked on my broken foot for two weeks before seeking medical care, embarrassed by the injury and convinced that it was merely a sprain. (Like my peers, I was convinced I could walk just fine.) Finally, one of my fellow American missionaries could no longer stand to see my foot so swollen and purple. She said three magic words: "Free medical care." Used to an American system, I had no idea that my Hong Kong I.D. gave me access to the X-rays I'd been avoiding. If only to prove her wrong about the damage, I went to the emergency room.

Like Hong Kong itself, the hospital was insanely crowded. I waited half a day for those free X-rays. During that time, a typhoon swept in, and a severe wind warning was "hoisted." I wasn't worried—it's hard to feel unsafe in a hospital emergency room. But when my X-rays were read and I was hustled off for a knee-to-toe cast, it was time to worry. The typhoon warning had alerted everyone to return home ASAP, and that meant nonemergency staff at the hospital too—which included the crutches department. So no crutches for me, and even with limited Cantonese, I understood that I should *absolutely not* put any weight on the cast *at all*.

So there I was with my enormous cast, sent home into a typhoon with one too-tall, old-fashioned crutch someone had found lying around. I called a neighbor to pick me up—the one who'd insisted that I get X-rays. I got home and collapsed on the couch, despairing about how to make dinner and get myself to bed when I could barely move.

I would have given anything for working crutches.

Which brings me to my friends who scoff at faith as a crutch: They imply that those who can walk just fine on their own should not stoop to using a crutch. Crutches, according to that opinion, are for lesser mortals—those who are broken.

But in fact, when I was broken and desperately needed crutches, it didn't make me feel like a lesser mortal. It made me feel mortal, period. I finally could see how all of us are broken in some way or another. The idea that only lesser mortals need faith says more about the proponents' anthropology than their theology. My anthropology says that human beings are hurting and hurtful people. We all bear the wounds and scars of life. None of us can walk well for long by our own power alone.

Various crutches are available, but some work better than others. Faith, spirituality, a connection to a Higher Power or something bigger than ourselves—those provide enough grace to move us along on the journey. A different kind of crutch doesn't: compulsive behaviors, addictive relationships, endless but temporary "self-help"—these only prop up our illusions of self-sufficiency temporarily.

A different anthropology

Coming face to face with all kinds of brokenness that year, I had Luther's theology and anthropology to help me understand it. Luther said that we live as both sinners and saints—as weak, broken human beings who are simultaneously justified—"sainted"—by God's grace. Luther was rooted in Saint Augustine's fourth-century theology, whose concept of original sin was behind Luther's concept of "sinner": We come into a flawed world with flaws of our own. Throughout our lives, we hurt others and are hurt ourselves, and we cannot pull *ourselves* out of this condition. Truly, we are *not* up to our journeys; they *will* require more than we can do or give or be.

But because of God's grace through Jesus, our insufficiency is not the end of the story. Luther spoke often of being "justified" by grace, which is a once-and-for-all act that Jesus accomplished through his death and resurrection. *Living* in grace, on the other hand, is the opposite: it happens in the embodied journeys of human lives. Part of that journey is figuring out what kind of journey it is.

My own story of living in grace began with the words carved on the front edge of the altar at Grace Lutheran Church where I grew up: "My grace is sufficient for you, for my power is made perfect in weakness" (2 Corin. 12:9). In church, grace was always in front of me, but outside the church I was learning something different: that one had to work hard for success, which would be followed by love. I worked hard to be perfect, lovable, and successful. Like Philip, I never believed it would be enough.

When I first started seminary, I tried to be perfect at ministry but was haunted by the sense that I was never good enough. I needed grace, but as Dietrich Bonhoeffer pointed out, I had two options: cheap grace and costly grace. A "cheap grace" response would have been, "Sure, I am enough—Jesus' love covers up all my faults." A "costly grace" response was harder: "It's true, I could never possibly be enough … but Jesus is." On the journey, a cheap grace response gives up and takes the easy way. A costly grace response jumps into the arms of Jesus and sees what grace will do next.

> *Clue:* Our anthropology and our theology often function in parallel. What do you believe about what is possible for people—what kind of resilience, healing, transformation? What role, if any, do you believe God plays in those?

Clues in weakness and failure

God's power may be made perfect in weakness, but when we are seeking our callings, our weaknesses are not usually where we tend to look. Our *strengths* are the best signposts to our calling, according to much secular and religious discernment literature. Look for your talents, they say, the things that come easy to you, the things you don't have to struggle with.

As we've seen, clues can indeed come in that form. But they don't always. If God's power is made perfect in weakness, then it may be precisely our weaknesses that point out how God is at work in and through us.

Writer Oriah Mountain Dreamer provides a refreshing contrast by pointing people to their weaknesses to find the "one word" they have been given to share with the world. "Look at your failures…. Look at what does not come easily to you, what you long for but find elusive. Think about what gets you into trouble…." She points out how this contrasts with so much of the guidance available: "You can feel how starting with your struggles and failures goes against the tendency of many New Age philosophies to start by looking at what you love and are good at."[2] Why look at our weaknesses to find the gifts we have to share? She says, "Because we cannot teach what we never had to learn…. The best teachers are those who have had to carefully and consciously learn how to do the thing they are teaching." Or, in the language of 2 Corinthians, our weaknesses are the places we see God's power at work most clearly.

I wonder now if that's why my Santa Clara colleagues and I told so many stories of our failures and wrong turns rather than stories of strengths, talents, and good choices. Part of this was humility, but it was also because our weaknesses and failures are often the places we could see the mystery of divine power at work. Painful experiences connect us to the human race—we are not "lesser mortals," but simply "mortal." Besides, how could we have taught discernment if we hadn't had to learn it ourselves?

Using our weaknesses

Sometimes God uses things we define as "weaknesses" in powerful ways. The story, *The Secret Garden*, is a charming example. Written in turn-of-the-twentieth-century England (and made into a movie in 1993), the story begins with ten-year-old Mary Lennox as a stubborn, selfish, and rather obnoxious little girl, deeply wounded by the death of her parents in India and her dislocation to England.[3] At the end of the story, she's still rather stubborn and selfish and a little bit obnoxious, though less wounded. Along the way, however, she contributes to some remarkable transformations in her sickly cousin and a neglected garden. The trans-formations aren't the result of her becoming a different person but of her being precisely the stubborn, selfish, and rather obnoxious person she is. As the story unfolds in the large and lonely house of her mostly absent uncle, Mary discovers her sickly cousin, Colin. "Everyone thinks I'll die," Colin tells Mary. She replies, "If everyone thought that about me, I wouldn't do it." With her stubbornness, she bullies him back to health.

I found grace in that movie during seminary, when I was trying to change myself into someone who could be a perfect minister. The movie was the kind of reminder I needed—and I needed them over and over—that God uses whoever we are in the moment to accomplish what needs doing. Often, we are changed in the process. Again, I needed lots of re-minders years later, when I was looking for a new call in ministry and fearing that my recent divorce might discourage a congregation from of-fering me a job. Grace came in the form of colleagues who reminded me that God could use even that painful experience to make me a better pas-tor. I didn't want to hear it at the time, but what I learned on my crutches was true of my divorce too: pain and the healing process join us with the human race. The challenge was, could I let grace be big enough to encompass even *that* experience?

> *Clue:* In The Secret Garden, Mary is forbidden to venture into the many unused rooms of the man-sion. Bored and curious, she ventures out anyway and even beyond the boundaries of the locked garden. Her "trespassing" becomes a means of grace when she discovers the garden and her cousin. When you are overly concerned about "doing things right," which perceived boundaries are you afraid of trespassing? How might that cut you off from the whole life God has in mind for you?

At work in the darkness

Our painful experiences, failures, fears of not being good enough, and weaknesses can hide clues. They can also become "baggage" that can weigh us down on the journey. Too often, we use our baggage and weaknesses as excuses. We ignore the clues telling us to try again where we have failed or to volunteer with those who share our particular pain. Too often, we despair that God could ever work any good out of it. But a God of possibility can use *anything* for good. So, instead of baggage, I've come to think of that pile of failures and fears as a compost pile in which we dump our psychic leftovers.

In composting, unseen transformation happens in deep, dark places. I was introduced to the idea as a member of the Lutheran Volunteer Corps. As part of the yearlong program, our community of seven was charged with living simply and practicing social justice in our daily lives. It was up to us to figure out the practical applications for running the household. Composting was not my idea, although it did make sense in theory. In practice, though, orange peels and coffee grounds and slimy stuff collected in a bucket in the kitchen, and since we never seemed to know whose turn it was to dump it in the backyard, it was usually overflowing and gathering flies.

I took my unenthusiastic turns at emptying the bucket onto the growing pile of muck, but other than that I tried to ignore the whole business. In the spring, I was surprised when a houseguest suggested he use the compost, now rich soil, to plant flowers in our front yard. I was astonished that all that garbage might actually prove useful.

Sure enough, one day I came home to geraniums in a planter along the sidewalk, but they only lasted a short time in the withering hot sun. Since none of us was motivated to remove them, they stayed in the planter until weeds started growing up among the dead plants. As the weeds grew, they revealed themselves not to be weeds at all, but cucumber and tomato plants. The seeds had survived the decomposition process intact.

I still compost years later, and I know now that seeds do this all the time. But at the time it seemed miraculous, and I clung to this remarkable image for my own treasure hunt. How many times had I followed the clues toward geraniums, and then feared for or watched their demise? And how many times had God grown vegetables in their place, something wonderful I had never planned for or imagined? Even more wonderful to me was how often those vegetables had emerged from a part of my past that I had considered useless. When I saw those cucumbers and toma- toes in our front yard, they gave me hope that even from my own internal "compost pile," God might call forth seeds of new life. Grace is *that* big.

Like most people, I suspect, I have my geraniums—the things I hope will be cultivated in my life. I imagine a certain set of gifts that I want to have, or at least be seen as having. Many of those will never grow very well out of my compost. With my personality, for example, I will simply never be The Best Listener Ever—a disappointing fact which I thought made me "not good enough" for ministry. But that doesn't mean I don't have *other* qualities helpful for ministry. Too many times I have mourned the geraniums and neglected to notice the vegetables growing instead. They are not always the gifts I want, but they are the ones I have. As with Mary Lennox, God can even use qualities I define as negative—stubbornness, for example. In calling us to see ourselves more and more as God sees us, grace calls us to look for and give thanks for those "vegetables."

Choices and character

The journey teaches us to recognize our *real* gifts and lets us get real about who we are and are becoming. As the treasure hunt has shown us, one thing leads to the next. Our experiences and choices lay the ground- work for the next set of choices. However, choices are not the only thing at work here. Over time, our choices form our *character*—who we are. When we appreciate how God uses those choices to form us, we start to see the journey differently. It's not so much about where we go and "what track we're on." Besides, we can't see enough of the picture to know if we're "on the right track" anyway. Rather, the journey is all about *who we become* along the way. When we use this ethic of character rather than an ethic of choice, we might ask this question less: "What should I do in this situation?" And we might ask this question more: "Who is this situation inviting me to become?"[4]

So we come back to the question: do our choices matter at all? I have struggled to answer that from my background. Lutheran theology emphasizes that we are saved by grace, not by works. Our choices and actions really don't matter to God's love for us, which could never be more or less than it already is. This is good news, but I missed this message: my choices might not affect my salvation, but they sure do affect the quality of my life.

C. S. Lewis understood this about daily choices and disciplines such as prayer. "Prayer doesn't change God," says his character in *Shadowlands*, a movie about Lewis' life. He explains to his friend, "That's not why I pray, Harry. I pray because I can't help myself. I pray because I'm helpless. I pray because the need flows out of me all the time, waking and sleeping. It doesn't change God, it changes me."[5] Annie Dillard develops this concept in her essay, "An Expedition to the Pole," in which she reflects on the habit of worship. Our choices work on us, rather than on God:

> You do not have to do these things; not at all. God does not,
> I regret to report, give a hoot. You do not have to do these
> things—unless you want to know God. They work on you, not
> on him.[6]

Does God give a hoot about our choices? In some ways, no: neither big decisions nor small daily choices can change how much God loves us. But in other ways, God *does* care: God wants us to have "abundant life." Often, I've found that the smaller choices matter for this even more than the big ones. Where I live or what job I have makes less difference than how I spend my energy each day; how I take care of my physical, emotional, spiritual, and mental health; and how I care for my relationships. Such choices can at times lead us away from God, and sometimes they can bring us closer. God may not "need" us to choose well, but our lives will be fuller and richer when we listen and try to make choices which will help draw us toward God.

Through our daily smaller choices, we practice being the person we will become—sometimes intentionally, sometimes unintentionally. Because we get really good at what we practice, we should pay attention to what we're practicing. For example, we might be perpetually stressed out and at the limits of busyness, dreaming of "someday" when we'll have time for family and friends and spiritual practice. In reality, we're getting further and further away from that ideal, because instead we're honing our skills of being stressed and busy. Or let's say you're in a job that chips away at your self-esteem and dignity day by day. You grudgingly decide to stay in the job and wait and see if something better comes along. But in the meantime, you get really good at being dissatisfied and perpetually frustrated—which makes it increasingly difficult to present yourself as a good candidate for "something better." On the other hand, if your discernment can lead you to see the job as practice in humility instead of an exercise in frustration, your eyes might be increasingly open to other opportunities where you could be of service. So your choices do make a difference—maybe not to God but to who you become.

> *Clue:* To see what you're practicing, look at your calendar or keep a journal of consolation and desolation. Attending to how your doing shapes your being gives you another tool for discernment: "What is this (job, relationship, home, city, community) inviting me to practice, and is that what I feel called to get good at?"

A big enough self

Under the infinitely wide umbrella of God's grace, what does it mean to draw closer to God and become who we are? Once we've accepted our compost and our real gifts, how can we tell if we're "becoming someone" on the journey?

Several years into ministry, I was reflecting on a similar question with some seminary classmates: what had we learned from our first few years of ministry? One friend described how he had been surprised to find himself taking a stand and speaking out where before he would have sat down and shut up. Another described how he had become more accepting of people's idiosyncrasies. Both seemed slightly surprised by the compassion and strength their vocation had drawn out of them. This is true in other vocations as well, when the journey itself effects the change. I've seen how parenting can draw qualities out of parents such as patience and responsibility; somehow parents can become "bigger" people than they were before.

Another friend told the story of the honor it was to care for his parents as they were dying. It brought him face to face with a love and spaciousness that he had never encountered. In becoming "big enough" to take it all in, he was permanently changed by the experience. All three of these stories tell me about doing the journey well: It means rising to the challenge and becoming a big enough person for the life you've been given. As we'll see in the next chapter, the process of formation means letting more space be created for love, beauty, and grace—more room to hold the divine, which can then be poured out for the sake of others.

Not everyone is up to that challenge at every one of life's invitations. Instead of stretching and growing, sometimes we shrink back and retreat into the known and the safe. I don't know what determines whether one becomes big enough or stays too small. But I do know that having a plan for how one's life is supposed to work out can make stretching and growing more difficult. I've encountered many young adults who not only have a plan but who also think that "doing adulthood right" *requires* a plan. As we've seen, there's nothing wrong with planning, but a master plan rarely accommodates all of life's surprises, and it often turns out to be too small for one's unique life. As a little girl, I had such a plan: getting married and having children. I couldn't imagine doing anything else. But the husband in the plan didn't materialize in my twenties. During that decade I was called to something else—work, graduate school, travel, friendship, and ministry. If my life hadn't diverged from my too-small plan, I would have missed out on all that life offered me. In fact, that decade of stretching and growing experiences gave me big enough courage to step up to the challenge of marriage in my thirties. Then, paradoxically and bittersweetly, the gifts of marriage helped me grow into compassion big enough to acknowledge the end of that relationship.

Each person's vocational journey holds a different combination of study, family, work, travel, interests, and surprises both welcome and not. For all of us, I believe, each growth experience makes us that much bigger to rise to the next challenge. "Growing up well" does not mean accomplishing your master plan. While there is satisfaction in doing what you set out to do—and often life does call us to that kind of determination—it can also keep us thinking way too small. So far I've learned this about how to do adulthood "right": first, you have to give up any notion of doing it "right."

In giving us abundant life, God wants for us not perfection but wholeness. When "staying on the right track" is the only guide, life remains too small, because grace invites us to something much bigger, wilder, and more lovingly whole. Grace invites us to embrace *everything* in our compost piles as potentially usable material for our formation: pain as well as joy, confusion as well as clarity. We are called to have a big enough heart to hold all the contradictions and challenges of living out vocation every day within our various roles and relationships. Wholeness means not cutting off the parts of you that don't fit but rather letting God draw them all into a self that's big enough for all your vocations. Grace gives us the courage to see the truth about ourselves and even to see clues in weakness and brokenness. We interpret what we find there by asking, "What might Jesus be doing with this?"

A funny thing happens as our selves become big enough to hold our weakness and brokenness compassionately. They become big enough to hold a community of other weak and broken people, too. Unlike self-sufficiency, faith gives me not only a God but also a community to lean on. That's what happened in that Hong Kong typhoon. As I was lying on the couch with my cast wondering how to make dinner without crutches, my church friends magically showed up *en masse* and swarmed into my kitchen to cook us all dinner. After the years I had invested in self-sufficiency, it was marvelous *and* difficult to sit back and receive their love and care. A community of faith was my crutch when I was literally broken. But even when my wounds are not visible, faith has often picked me up and helped me walk with dignity. Faith may be a crutch—but it's one I believe we all need. Grace means the difference between life and death—between being weak and yet able to move through the sustaining Spirit, and being weak without resources.

In an offertory hymn at a church I used to attend, we would sing just before Communion, "We are poor, but we've brought ourselves the best we could."[7] I envisioned people limping to the table to receive Communion, with their weakness and wounds made visible and representing so much sin and hurting. We came to the table to beg for healing, forgiveness we could never earn or deserve, and grace to make us whole. That summer in Hong Kong, as I limped to Communion on my crutches, I finally got it. Those wounds are the very places where God's love and power, made perfect in weakness, can fill us. We may not come away from the table cured, but we come away healed, reconciled, and strengthened for the journey.

No, the journey is definitely not about perfection; grace is most evident in weakness and in the darkness of composting garbage. So what *is* it about? Practice.

> **Clue:** Many have pointed out that the word "human" shares with "humility" the root word "humus": dirt. Perhaps this can help us have a sense of humor about our weaknesses and failures. Which of yours do you struggle most to accept?

Further exploration

On patience:

• All kinds of meditation help with patience. I particularly like meditative chants such as the ones from the Taizé Community in France www.taize.fr/en. Two of my favorites are "Our Darkness" and "Come and Fill Our Hearts." You can also find Taizé prayer music on iTunes.
• *Sabbath: Finding Rest, Renewal, and Delight in Our Busy Lives,* by Wayne Muller, suggests practices for "slowing down" and connecting with God, oneself, and others (New York: Bantam Books, 1999).

On building character:

• The film *The Ultimate Gift* is an example of very intentional character-building through a series of tasks, laid out by a grandfather for his grandson (The Ultimate Gift LLC, 2006).
• Programs like Outward Bound claim that "adventure-based education" develops character: www.outwardbound.org.

On a big enough self:

• In the film, *Big Fish*, a dying man's son tries to assemble reality out of the stories his father had told of his life. Can his life really be as "big" as the "fish stories" he has told? (Columbia Pictures, 2003).
• In her books *The Invitation, The Call,* and *The Dance,* Oriah Mountain Dreamer writes powerfully and provocatively of her own vocational experience and others' (New York: HarperCollins, 1999, 2001, and 2003, respectively). Her poem which begins *The Invitation* calls readers to a big enough self. She writes, "I want to know if you will risk looking like a fool for love, for your dream, for the adventure of being alive."

FINDING YOURSELF

SEVEN

Formed by Practice

What if the events of our history are molding us as a sculptor molds his clay, and if it is only in a careful obedience to these molding hands that we can discover our real vocation and become mature people?
—Henri J. M. Nouwen[1]

ONCE OUR ATTENTION has been turned toward character more than choices, we discover new questions. Instead of asking whether our journey is getting us anywhere, we ask, "Is my journey making me anyone?" The journey reveals ourselves in a new way: as people who are always being created and recreated by God, through a process known as "formation." There is much good news in the concept of formation, not least of which is the theological middle ground it offers between the black and white of "God has nothing to do with our choices" and "God has all our choices planned." Formation introduces us to the hands-on work of the God of possibility—the work of an Artist, and particularly of a potter.

Earthen vessels

Isaiah 64:8 says, "O Lord, you are our Father; we are the clay, and you are our potter; we are all the work of your hand." A potter is a fitting image for one whose material begins as clay, as Genesis says humans do. Like a clay vessel, our work is to become big enough for our lives and to welcome greater capacities for love, joy, service, surrender—all the things we are called to "pour out" for the sake of the world. Paul says in

2 Corinthians that we are earthen vessels, or in some translations, "clay jars" (or "crackpots"!) He also reminds us in that verse that what we hold is, indeed, "treasure"—the light of Christ. "We have this treasure in clay jars," he writes, "so that it may be made clear that this extraordinary power belongs to God and does not come from us" (2 Corin. 4:7). Jars of clay—not very glamorous materials: "The Lord God formed man from the dust of the ground, and breathed into his nostrils the breath of life" (Gen. 2:7). As others have noted, we are basically divinely inspired dirt, shaped by the hands of the potter not just once but throughout our lives.

"Formation" is the process by which we take on the shape that God is fashioning in our personality, experiences, work, relationships, and life. This term is more familiar in some traditions than in others. In some, it is more common to think of oneself as a "tool" that God *uses* rather than as a "vessel" that God *shapes* and *fills*.[2] A tool is an apt metaphor in an ethic of choice, because it asks, "What do you want me to do?" Appropriate to an ethic of character, a vessel inquires, "What shape do you want me to be, and what do you want me to hold?" We see this shift from tool to vessel, from doing to being, as our attention turns from choices to character.

God the potter

It is sometimes said that the beginning of vocation discernment is the desire to be of service, the desire to be useful. When you're dealing with clay on a potter's wheel, however, there's a lot that needs to happen before you end up with a useful vessel.

First, the clay has to be prepared before it is centered on the wheel and stretched into its shape. In the preparation process called wedging, the clay gets folded over on itself repeatedly and turned inward. Spiritual disciplines have a similar effect on us, as they invite us inward to see ourselves as God's works of art, loved into existence by a creator still at work on us. We are being prepared for the shape God has in mind for us. But this "preparation" never really ends; the repeated call to repentance in the Bible reminds us that we are never finished products. We always have opportunities to be reshaped—or, in theological language, to "repent" or turn around. The artistic process goes on during our whole lives.

We are invited to trust the Artist, but not *only* the Artist. I am reminded of an introductory ceramics class I took many years ago. My perfec-
tionism made it very difficult for me; I would get hung up on every single
one of those stages of a vessel. I was convinced that the clay was never
going to do what I wanted it to do. In particular, wedging drove me crazy.
I'd been warned that if you don't wedge the clay properly, air bubbles
remain in the clay and then when you put the finished pot in the very
hot kiln, the air expands and breaks the pot. I was positive that no matter
how hard I worked on the clay, my pots would eventually break. So I was
very pessimistic through the whole process. First, I didn't trust myself as
an inexperienced artist. But I also didn't trust the clay.

I didn't realize that until years later, watching an accomplished potter
throw a pot. He trusted the clay, and it showed. It's hard to describe an
artist working with materials that he or she loves. Maybe you've seen a
cabinetmaker with wood or a chef with food. No matter what the materials, when you watch an artist you can see almost a reverence for them,
a trust that they are what they are and that they can become what the
artist intends. There's also a recognition that the material has limits and
a willingness to experiment. And there's a hope, even an expectation, of
being surprised and delighted.

God is that kind of artist with the materials of our lives. So we're invited to entrust our lives to God, a decision we get to make over and over
again—every time we start to think that we're the master artist. When I
begin to think I'm in charge of the artistic process, soon I'm seeing my
life the way I used to fight with those poor pots—whatever I do, it will
probably blow up. I become convinced that the materials are so impossible and so stubborn and so flawed that they can never take the shape
intended for them. Often, I still don't trust the clay. How can the frail and
flawed material of *human* life possibly take part in a *divine* purpose? How
can *we* become a vessel for *God's* love? These are good questions for an
incarnational faith. The good news is that God not only *creates* human
beings, God also *becomes* one in Jesus. The birth of Jesus answered the

question once and for all: YES, human life is enough to hold the divine. When you trust the materials of your life and the divine Artist at work on them, it leaves no room for anxiety. Paul writes with exuberant joy in his letter to the Christians at Philippi:

I thank my God every time I remember you. In all my prayers for all of you, I always pray with joy because of your partner-ship in the gospel from the first day until now, being confident of this, that he who began a good work in you will carry it on to completion until the day of Christ Jesus (Phil. 1:3–6, NIV).

You are still under construction, he tells them. You're still being shaped by the divine Artist, and that won't come to an end until the world does. Paul trusts that they will be shaped into vessels for God's love, which can be poured out for the sake of the world.

And this is my prayer: that your love may abound more and more in knowledge and depth of insight, so that you may be able to discern what is best and may be pure and blameless until the day of Christ, filled with the fruit of righteousness that comes through Jesus Christ—to the glory and praise of God (Phil. 1:9–11, NIV).

That is my hope for all of us who want the joy and peace that comes from letting go of shaping ourselves. We are clay in God's hands. Our job is to welcome, celebrate, and cooperate with the work of God in ourselves, in one another, and in our communities, trusting that the One who began a good work in us will bring it to completion.

Clue: With which materials do you work best? Which ones are most difficult for you? If you were a kind of "raw material" on which God works (wood, words, ice, math equations, whatever), what would you be?

The slow, gentle work of God

One season of the church year in particular calls our attention to repentance and to God's work on us and our character: the season of Lent, the forty days leading up to Easter. I've always loved Lent, but what I love about it has changed. I used to love the austerity of it, this idea that I could take on (or give up) something out of the ordinary and change the shape of my life. I romanticized the notion that God was going to do something radical in my life in those forty days. It was going to be difficult, and it might even hurt a little—but that's how I'd know it was good for me.

Lots of people identify with an image of a God whose love can hurt, even when it's good for us. There seems to be something attractive, or perhaps just recognizable from human experience, about a "tough-love" God. Perhaps it's the same idea as a calling that costs something and thus is worth something. However, in recent years my own physical "clay" has introduced me to a much more gentle and patient experience of God.

Leading up to Lent of 2003, my spine was signaling me that it was weakening. I'd had scoliosis since I was a preteen, and finally the pain had come, just as predicted by my first physical therapist. My back held together for thirty years without much attention, for which I am grateful. But that winter it gave notice. One day I bent over, and the sharp pain told me that I was low maintenance no longer. By the time I saw a chiropractor, I really needed help—but my back was so stressed that it couldn't withstand much "helping." So I faced a dilemma: I was supposed to exercise to regain some flexibility, but even the stress of walking was too much. She prescribed walking in the swimming pool. It helped, but it was extremely slow progress.

Instead of this time-consuming regimen, I would have greatly preferred something like the titles I find on amazon.com: *7 Steps to a Pain-Free Life, 8 Steps to Create the Life You Want,* or *The 9 Steps to Financial Freedom.*[3] Every now and then I would complain to my chiropractor that I wanted the quick-fix treatment, not the 1,936-step version. No such luck. She was about as receptive as God has been when I pray for quick fixes and get answers that involve a long haul. But the long haul contains much grace: it is often much more gentle. It reminds me of God's unfailing patience. And for those times when I feel so fragile I can hardly stand to be helped, one gentle step at a time feels just right.

> *Clue:* In John 2:1–11, Jesus changes water into wine at a wedding party. Notice the importance of vessels in this story: "Now standing there were six stone water jars ..." How does the story sound different if you imagine the vessel as a character in the story? How do your choices look if you imagine *yourself* as the vessel, ready to be touched by Jesus' transformation?

Willing to change shape

Over time, the work on my spine has the potential to literally change my shape. But this work is not done from scratch, and neither is God's work on us. None of us starts as a smooth lump of clay, ready to be perfectly formed. Most of us, by the time we are aware of ourselves, have been "de-formed" spiritually, psychologically, or emotionally. We might be deformed by a traumatic event or simply by struggles with our family of origin. We get deformed by the sins and shortcomings that plague human life—self-centeredness, hubris, anxiety, addictions. Whether we are deformed by outside events or internal disorder, all of us come to faith formation rather bent out of shape.

Over time, most of us get rather good at being bent and twisted in particular ways. Our habits are what we practice, and we get good at them. I can see this now in the bends and twists of my back, which tend to get worse over time. My body essentially "practices" being crooked. I practice another kind of deformation when I am self-centered or afraid. I picture a metaphorical crookedness in Romans, where Paul says, "Do not be conformed to this world" (Rom. 12:2). He says that if you practice what the world practices, then you will take on its shape. You will get good at the same bends and twists of self-centeredness, hubris, anxiety, addictions.

Paul's solution for the community in Rome sounds simple: "Be transformed by the renewing of your minds." Traditionally, Christians have had many ways of talking about transformation. Some emphasize the dramatic transformation of conversion and being "born again." Others emphasize a more gradual re-formation over time. We need both those models, which have in common Jesus and his work through the Holy Spirit. Without the re-formation over time and the practicing of new faithful habits, a dramatic conversion isn't likely to stick. However, without conversion to inspire those new habits and give a glimpse of their possibility, a gradual approach may not be strong enough to yank us out of the old grooves with an alternative to the "pattern of the world."

I've seen this recently in my physical therapist's and chiropractor's approaches to the bends and twists in my back. The re-formation is certainly gradual through daily exercises in which my back "practices" being straighter, and the muscles strengthen and stretch in new ways. But there is also the dramatic change of regular adjustments which give me a glimpse of a new shape. The adjustments don't stick without the exercises, and the exercises don't provide enough change on their own. It seems I need *both* the dramatic transformations *and* the gradual re-formation.

It is tempting to replace all these kinds of powerful formation (trans-, con-, and re-) with mere *in*formation, of which there is no shortage in our culture. Information rarely has the same long-term effect on our hearts and lives but can act as a quick and easy substitute, silencing the deeper question: am I willing to change shape, or am I determined to stay deformed in the ways I've practiced so well?

What if someone came along and completely transformed your life for you? That's what Jesus does for the woman (or what he does *to* her) in the story of Luke 13:10–17, often referred to as The Bent-Over Woman. She has been crippled for eighteen years, Luke tells us, not able to straighten up at all. During that time, her infirmity would have shaped her routine, her relationships, and her view of the world. (How do you see the sky from that position? Or look into someone's face?) One day she comes into the synagogue, and Jesus is teaching there. The story doesn't say that she came looking for healing or that she asked for it. Suddenly she is called forward, Jesus lays his hands on her, and then she is free. Luke says, "Immediately she stood up straight and began praising God" (v. 13).

Her life has just changed irrevocably, apparently through no request of her own. From the way she prepares her meals to the way she looks at her surroundings to the way people look at her—all will be different from now on. To praise God in that moment would be remarkable, a sign of trust that the accompanying changes will be good ones. But are we always so trusting? We humans can get pretty attached to the status quo—even when it is uncomfortable, and even though we may long for relief. Deep down we often prefer a discomfort and deformation we know how to handle rather than a relief accompanied by discomforts yet unknown.

One of the problems of trying to change the status quo is the fact that we can never alter just *one* thing. Instead, one action often creates a ripple effect, sending change spinning out of control. One clue follows another; one choice opens up another set of choices. For systems that prefer stasis, that's irritating at best and panic-inducing at worst, even with *positive* changes. Change one thing about your life, or family, or workplace, and the system will probably try to change it back and make you conform again to your old shape.

Just ask an alcoholic who gets sober. Her family may be so used to the twisted shape of addiction that even the ones who once longed for her sobriety may now find themselves inadvertently sabotaging her recovery.

Just ask someone who finds a long-term workplace suddenly intolerable after some counseling taught him to "stand up straight."

Or just ask my physical therapist about the stasis in my back. Sure, it hurts sometimes, but this is a discomfort it knows how to handle. Change the shape even a little, and the muscles try to get it to change back. They complain a lot through aches and pains. And having undergone the uncomfortable ripple effects of other positive changes in my life, I understand completely.

> *Clue:* Who in your life—family, friends, work—depends on you continuing certain habits?

Everyday clues and disciplines

God works through gradual reformation and dramatic transformation in everyday choices and circumstances, not only in big decisions. Sometimes our clues refer to small choices, not big ones. For example, a feeling of dissatisfaction with one's job *may* be a clue to change jobs, *or* it may be a clue to change one's daily routine to make room for a more joyful activity. Clues may point to how we spend our time and use our energy, and with whom, on a daily basis. Sometimes this kind of choice can shape us most, like a stream of water reshaping a rock through erosion over centuries. The same principles of the treasure hunt hold true, as we pay attention and allow one thing to unfold into the next in a creative and helpful way.

Some years ago, a little Astroturf provided a small clue that led to big changes in my daily life. A journey of small steps led to a complete health overhaul, from exercise to medical care to diet. In my first call in ministry, I had moved into my first solo apartment. It was on the second floor and had a small concrete balcony. As I lived there for a few months, I felt called to garden. As incongruous as it was with the concrete floor, I kept envisioning lawn on the balcony. So I covered the concrete in Astroturf and added potted plants, and it was just right. But then the garden clued me in to a need for a fountain. With the fountain in place, I kept imagining how much a cat would enjoy the garden. With a lifetime of allergies, I'd never had a pet, but I began to research it anyway and decided to try an adult cat. Within weeks, an announcement appeared in our church bulletin: an elderly woman had to give up her two-year-old orange tabby.

In a wonderful "outside clue," the church secretary pointed it out to me: "Weren't you talking about getting a cat?" I followed up on the clue, and the cat and I hit it off. Appropriately, Max moved in with me on Epiphany. Less than two weeks later, I threw out my back for good when I picked him up. (No doubt something else would have eventually broken the camel's back, so to speak, but Max provided the unavoidable clue.) A friend's recommendation led me to a chiropractor, and we began the journey of rehabilitation which has transformed my life more than almost any "big decision" I've ever made. In fact, it may even have opened doors to a big decision; sometimes I wonder if I could have let my marriage end when it did without first having spent several years learning to care for the health of my body, mind, and spirit.

Part of that care was in the form of spiritual disciplines, which are powerful opportunities for God to work on us. Disciplines such as reading Scripture, communal worship and sacraments, prayer, service, and meditation all shape us over time. But we're invited to do them without any promise of eventual accomplishment or flawlessness. In this case, practice does not make perfect. It makes ... practiced. It's a little like the efforts to reshape my crooked back. Those efforts, too, require much persistence and promise no perfection. The widely accepted medical wisdom has been that scoliosis can't be corrected without surgery. Even the most optimistic professionals tell me that the most successful combination of chiropractic adjustment and daily exercise is unlikely to straighten out the curves in my back much at all. Similarly, even for the most optimistic theologian, it is widely accepted that humans cannot live perfect lives, with no bends and twists of sin and frailty. We can't possibly stay on the right track ourselves. So why would we put ourselves through spiritual disciplines of prayer, reading Scripture, service, and worship if we can't reshape the bends and twists of our selves?

For one thing, *without* those disciplines, our bends and twists will get even worse. As with spines, we become what we practice, and without intentional re-formation, we'll get very good at those *de*-formations. But an even better reason is that *with* those disciplines, our "shape" can improve. In spiritual lives as in spines, even a little less pain and suffering, and a little more serenity and energy, are worth the attention and effort.

Stretching and strengthening

It's not just any effort that helps. We are all "de-formed" in different ways, and our disciplines must address those particularities. Otherwise, we may actually keep practicing the same deformations. For example, long before I first saw a chiropractor, I used to do yoga. I was very good at stretching the muscles that stretched easily and strengthening those that were already strong. I didn't know how to pay attention to the cramped and weaker muscles that demanded more effort than I knew how to give. In a similar way, my main spiritual discipline used to be journaling; I would analyze my thoughts and insights in a very private space. Through that practice (which was somewhat helpful to me and is very helpful for many), I was strengthening those already strong "muscles" of analysis and privacy, while paying far less attention to weaker areas such as expressing spontaneous emotion in community.

This new awareness of particular "curves" has made it much harder to suggest spiritual disciplines to others. How should I know which ways people are "bent," and which "muscles" they need to strengthen in order to re-form? No universal advice seems to work anymore. "Take time alone" doesn't work for people who are isolated. "Focus on community" isn't helpful for people who are so outward-focused that they don't listen to God speaking within themselves. To reshape the curve in my spine, I practiced stretching the tighter muscles and strengthening the weaker ones. People could do the same thing with their unique spiritual curves. Some people would grow spiritually if they became less self-centered and served others more. Others are so focused on others' needs that they would do better to know themselves and their own God-given desires. To say to *all*, "Serve others more" or "Focus on yourself" risks strengthening people where they are already strong and ignoring the places where they are weak.

Then how do we know if we should speak up more or keep our mouths shut and listen? Become more vulnerable or concentrate on our own safety? These too are questions for discernment, in which we attend to God's work on our particular, unique lives. A spiritual director is invaluable here—or anyone, regardless of title, who is devoted to listening contemplatively to God's work in you. Generally, a holy discomfort is a good sign that we're getting out of our well-practiced grooves and exercising a new shape. It helps to remember that experimentation is allowed here; formation is a lifelong process, and God's grace covers all our imperfect efforts. In fact, with God's help those efforts may bring about far more than we imagine or deserve, reshaping us far beyond what we could accomplish ourselves.

> *Clue:* Dietrich Bonhoeffer writes in his book on Christian community: *"Let him who cannot be alone beware of community*.... But the reverse is also true: *Let him who is not in community beware of being alone."*[4] How do you know which one you need, and when?

Living vocationally

When we attend to the ways God works on us through daily practice and discipline, even the meaning of "vocation" begins to shift. Vocation is commonly understood as the grammatical noun it is: a person, place, or thing (work, relationship, commitment) to which one is "called." But most people have many vocations during their lifetimes, often living multiple vocations simultaneously (son or daughter, worker, parent, student, spouse, citizen, friend, among others). I've found it helpful to think of vocation as if it were an adverb rather than a noun. When vocation is thought of as an adverb, it highlights a *way* of living life rather than a static place or set path. I've come to understand it more as "living vocationally," in which you make daily choices with integrity and faith. It's a way of living that allows you to keep putting one foot in front of the other on the treasure hunt, trusting God to lead the way.

Like most things worth doing, living vocationally is difficult to measure. It's not what I pictured when I was the age of my students, trying to figure out how to become an adult correctly. I wanted to find my vocation and get the Adulthood Stamp of Approval. But vocation cannot be achieved, it can only be practiced. It means attending to our choices and the clues within and outside us, with attention to how God is changing our shape to become a vessel big enough for our unfolding life. When we follow the clues to the places God wants to work on us, we are living vocationally. Often, those "places" are communities.

> *Clue:* How can you tell if you're "living vocationally"? Other adverbs can help flesh this out: faithfully, congruently, authentically, with integrity, according to one's best self.... What terms work for your understanding?

Further exploration

On vessels:

- In Rachel Naomi Remen's book, *Kitchen Table Wisdom*, the chapter called "The Container" tells the story of a wounded young man who pictures both his injury and his eventual healing as a broken vessel (New York: Riverhead Books, 1996), 114–118.
- The hymn, "Lord, Speak to Us That We May Speak" (also called "Lord, Speak to Me"), by Frances R. Havergal (1872), envisions people as vessels filled by God and poured out for others in their speaking, feeding, teaching, leading, and other actions. You can find the words and tune at http://nethymnal.org.

On the slow, gentle work of God:

- "Above all, trust in the slow work of God" begins the famous poem of the French Jesuit priest Pierre Teilhard de Chardin (1881–1955). You can find it in *Hearts on Fire: Praying with Jesuits* (Michael Harter, S.J., ed., Chicago: Loyola Press, 2004), 102–103, online at http://issuu.com/loyolapress/docs/hearts_on_fire.
- *Practicing Our Faith: A Way of Life for a Searching People*, edited by Dorothy C. Bass, looks at specific formative practices such as hospitality, household economics, and forgiveness (San Francisco: Jossey-Bass, 1997).
- The two parallel plots of the film *Sliding Doors* offer an interesting meditation on the effects of one seemingly insignificant change in circumstance and the various choices it makes available (Intermedia Films, 1998).

EIGHT

Discerning Community

God alone is free enough of wounds to offer us a fearless space.
—Henri J. M. Nouwen[1]

HOW DO WE COOPERATE with God's shaping work? For one thing, we can put ourselves in places God can work on us. We choose places where we can practice the things we are called to get good at—things like compassion, forgiveness, and tolerance, as well as particular talents. We can ask ourselves, when evaluating potential clues, "Where might God want to work on me?" The answer is usually a community, but the possibilities for a "community of formation" are endless. It could be a community for working, volunteering or serving, learning, worshiping, loving—or all of the above. All kinds of places can function as the Potter's wheel.

Earlier in this book, we saw community as a means to self-realization and self-fulfillment. Now, we'll look at it the other way around: vocation is a way of putting yourself in the service of community—pouring out the contents of the vessel, so to speak. The pouring, in turn, continues to reveal the shape and use of the vessel.

Path vs. place

In Luther's writing, vocation is commonly pictured as a *place* God finds you. I didn't find this image particularly helpful when I was faced with choices about vocation: I thought I had to choose just the right place where I would ideally stay forever. Within the parameters of his time and his theology, Luther didn't have much concept of choices or movement. (He may have experienced them, however, when he turned away from the law his father had wanted him to study and entered religious life instead.) A notion of "place" may be helpful for sustaining the sense that God is all around, but the metaphor is too settled to compare to the mobility of so many young adults. That's why, in my own vocation discernment, I had adopted the notion of a "spiritual journey" from writers and theologians from a variety of backgrounds, including Christian and New Age. Seeing my life as a *path* unfolding through various decisions made sense to my life as a college student and as a seminarian. But the further I went on my own journey, the more I found myself needing something that could *sustain* a calling, not just help me *choose* one. I needed something that would help me to see God's work in a given place over time. Now I've found myself reaching back in my own tradition for a concept of "place," which reminds me how much more God cares about who I am becoming than about what I choose specifically.[2]

When I started work on the Santa Clara discernment project, I was the only project staffer who was not Catholic. When we shared our own traditions of vocation, I often felt like a fish out of water. In one conversation focused on the significance of people's decisions to their vocational "path," the project director asked me, "What would Luther say about this?" I had been struggling to make such a connection, but this point struck me: "He'd say, 'Look around you—that's your vocation.' " Even as students were following the path of clues on their treasure hunts, at the same time they were looking around to notice the places God was already at work on them in their roles as student, friend, citizen, sibling, and other roles. Later, colleagues told me, "Every time a student says, 'My vocation is to be a student,' I recognize a Lutheran influence."

Another experience there illustrated a similar connection. A leader of the project, a Jesuit, was invited to give a lunchtime talk to faculty and staff about *sustaining* a vocation. This was intentionally distinguished from *choosing* a vocation, as the students were doing. The project's goal of helping faculty and staff discern their vocations along with students assumed that they wouldn't necessarily discern a new career outside the university! This talk was a chance to emphasize that vocations are not only chosen; some are also sustained over time. I had heard this speaker on a number of occasions, and few people were as inspiring and articulate as he was about Ignatian approaches to vocation discernment. However, listening to him talk about sustaining a vocation, I could have sworn that he had suddenly become a Lutheran. He spoke of God's presence in daily life, which is a principle found in Ignatian spirituality as well as Lutheran. Ignatius called it "finding God in all things," but Luther probably would have turned it around, as this Jesuit now did. He spoke of *God* finding *us* through our work and relationships. We don't need to "escape" our daily lives in order to find God. (Though Luther and Ignatius were on opposite sides of the Reformation, they agreed on this point and imagined different ways to bring religious life out of monasteries, where it was separate from people's daily lives and work.)

I finally understood why I'd been so stymied by using Lutheran theology to make vocational choices as a young adult: it is not made for *choosing* vocations, it's made for *sustaining* them. We need both approaches on the treasure hunt. Remember Anne Lamott's idea of the spiritual journey as a series of "staggers between lily pads"? I appreciate this image for many reasons, especially for the way it combines the images of path— even if it resembles "staggering"—and place, the lily pads themselves. We need to attend both to the journey *between* "lily pads" and to the formative experience *in* each place: "How is God working on me here?"

> *Clue:* Who has shaped you? In other words, who have you tried to be like, consciously or unconsciously? Who have you tried *not* to be like? Think of heroes, role models, and authority figures, and don't forget family members and peers.

Placed

In John 15:16, Jesus tells his disciples, "You did not choose me but I chose you. And I appointed you to go and bear fruit." "Appointed" is the Greek word *tithemi*, which also means simply "put." God "puts" us in places where we can bear fruit; our job in following clues is to look for those places—places where we can not only "be fulfilled" but also be of service. A vessel, after all, is meant for pouring out.

One of the "places" I considered after graduation from college was further academic study. The problem was, I couldn't figure out which field to enter; I had combined multiple disciplines—history, religion, literature—in my college major of American Studies, and any of them seemed worthy of further study. Bemoaning my confusion to a professor one day, I expected him to advise me on the pros and cons of different fields. I expected him to talk about choices. Instead, he approached the question from the perspective of character and community. "Well," he asked me, "who do you want to hang around with?" Different disciplines have different cultures, he pointed out—something I had seen already at my own college. I suspect he was asking where I saw myself fitting in best, but after "hanging around with" the church now for a while, I see that there's more to it than fitting. There is also *shaping*. "Who you hang around with" determines what you'll practice, either through imitation or in reaction. We might be shaped through the habits we pick up, as one picks up an accent or starts walking in step with another person. Or we might be shaped in reaction to something we *don't* want to become.

While communities do shape us in different ways, God can use *any* kind of relationship to shape us into our best selves. As we saw from *The Secret Garden*, even our idiosyncrasies and defects can call the best out of another person, the same way that Mary and Colin's stubbornness and selfishness called the best out of each other. In *Amazing Grace*, Kathleen Norris tells of a friend who compares the intimacy of monastic community to a rock tumbler. "It's great," her friend says, "if you want to come out nice and polished."[3] Community smoothes out the rough edges and brings out the shine.

Mirroring the beautiful

Communities shape us in many ways, and especially by the way they see us. A helpful community of formation does two things well: 1) it sees an individual as a whole, integrated person, not just as a particular role, and 2) it is invested not only in who we were and are, but also in who we are becoming. Similar to contemplative listening, a community of formation watches for what hasn't been born yet. Such a community can be hard to find, and precious when we encounter one. We rarely see each other so holistically; usually we just see the side of someone who's a team member or an employee, and not as a daughter or brother or parent, for example.

We cooperate with our own formation when we allow ourselves to be seen for all of who we are, which can be a frightening proposition. It's common to believe, consciously or unconsciously, "If people *really* knew me (what I think, what I feel, who I am), they would reject me." That assumes people knowing us at our worst, seeing our faults and brokenness. With that assumption, we become vulnerable to rejection when we let someone see our worst, the "real" self that we'd rather keep hidden. But defining our worst as our "real" self is somewhat arbitrary and pessimistic. Perhaps we are so careful to be realistic that we see the glass as half empty rather than half full, attentive to the worst rather than the best. "When we find people's flaws after a long acquaintance with them, we believe we are finally seeing the truth about them," Robert Bondi writes in *To Love as God Loves*.[4] She contrasts this modern perspective with a much earlier tradition: "Our Christian ancestors thought exactly the opposite: we see people as they really are only when we see them through the tender and compassionate eyes of God." So who's to say that our "real" self is not the *best* of who we are? Maybe, if we could see from the Creator's perspective, we would see our God-given gifts as who we "really" are.

Certainly, people need relationships in which they find acceptance even for their worst. In a Christian context, that's what confession and absolution are for: bringing to light the things we'd rather keep hidden, and assuring each other of love and forgiveness. But with Bondi's perspective, I don't want to stop with accepting the worst. I want to be part of a community that sees the best in people, receives their God-given gifts, and celebrates the signs of the Creator in their lives.

However, this does not eliminate the fear of rejection. After all, our best selves can be rejected too. Back in junior high and high school, when my mom and others said, "Just be yourself," their advice was supposed to *calm* my fears. Instead, it ramped them up. It was "myself" I feared having rejected, by the eyes of peers and teachers more analytical and critical than "tender and compassionate." Revealing one's best requires even more vulnerability than disclosing the worst. To be rejected for one's worst would be no great surprise; deep down, we expect this anyway. But what if our *best* isn't good enough or doesn't fit in? Then we're *really* in trouble. To unveil the best of ourselves—to offer our deepest love, present our greatest talent, or share our most unique gift—is to risk everything.

In a relationship, it is indeed painful when the other person cannot tolerate our faults and brokenness. But it is truly excruciating when the other person cannot receive our giftedness. This is true not only in romantic relationships or friendships but also in living out our callings, in which we offer what we have to a community and hope it is needed and accepted. Speaking on vocation discernment, Father Michael Himes of Boston College has compared that vulnerability to the risk of "unrequited love"—arguably one of the most painful kinds of rejection.[5]

However, when our gifts *are* received and our best *is* seen, it can be a profoundly formative experience. In her book *Notes on the Need for Beauty*, Ruth Gendler says that people become more beautiful as you get to know them.[6] She is commenting on our changed seeing, but I wonder if it's a self-fulfilling process, if people also grow into the way they are seen. If they are seen as beautiful, perhaps they become even more beautiful. People are loved into change far more often than they are nagged or persuaded or suggested into it.

That's the way Jesus sees and transforms. In Mark's gospel, we hear several times that Jesus "looked around." Particularly notable is the way he looks at a rich young man, just before he tells the man that in order to follow him, the man should sell all he has and give it to the poor. Mark writes, "Jesus, looking at him, loved him" (Mark 10:21). In ancient times people thought that seeing happened by light going out from the eyes rather than light coming in. Seeing was something that happened out beyond the person, when the eye's light hit the object. When Jesus looks around, Mark probably understands something to be coming out of his eyes: love. When Jesus looks at us, he loves us.

What would it be like to be part of a community where people could look at each other with love coming out of their eyes? One thing is for sure: we would not have to be afraid to be seen, really seen. In her book *A Return to Love*, Marianne Williamson has a well-known passage often quoted in the context of becoming one's best. She too suggests that it may be harder to become our best than to show our worst. "Our deepest fear is not that we are inadequate. Our deepest fear is that we are powerful beyond measure." However, she says, it's not only our opportunity but also our responsibility to show our best: "Your playing small does not serve the world. There is nothing enlightened about shrinking so that other people won't feel insecure around you." After all, showing one's own best can encourage others to do the same: "As we let our own light shine, we unconsciously give other people permission to do the same."[7]

> *Clue:* In learning to supervise others, I've been told that people learn more from seeing what's going *right*, rather than always having the *wrong* pointed out. I wonder if that tactic could work on ourselves, too, when we are tempted to focus on what's wrong. What's going right in your life these days?

Choosing community

Not all communities are capable of loving in this way; neither are all
friendships, marriages, or significant relationships, all of which I include
under the umbrella of "community." Most of us will experience unrequited love more than once in our lives, in communities which can't accept our "light," our giftedness, or our growing and changing over time.
Sometimes community asks us to shrink to fit in or requires us to leave
a significant portion of ourselves behind, rather than calling us to be a
bigger person. Those can all be important clues to move on to a different
community where God can work on you. On the other hand, clues may
also help us decide to stay and change the things we can; sustaining a vocation over time (including sustaining relationships) has many of those
moments of "discernment-in-place."

When you're discerning whether to leave a particular community, be
careful: Too often in our exceedingly mobile society, we give up on a
community too quickly and think a new one will be better. This is what
we're trained to do with all kinds of products and services, as American
culture trains us to be savvy consumers. But if we're just a "consumer" of
community, our best and our gifts can never be seen and received.

You might notice consumerism at work when you hear or say, "I'm
not getting much out of this." I hear this sometimes in relation to the
community I pastor, though I don't often hear it directly. Usually it's
admitted reluctantly, and often in the third person: "They left because
they weren't getting much out of that community/worship/Bible study/
and so on." Don't get me wrong: I appreciate that many people need to
"shop around" for a tradition and community that fit. I celebrate the way
people are driven to keep seeking and following clues until something
satisfies their longings. I just don't believe that people's deepest longings
can be satisfied by merely getting something out of an experience. For a
consumer of any goods or services, there is just the transaction: payment
for something you receive. "Consumers" don't give and receive love.

We've already seen how we become what we practice. If we practice
being a consumer, we will end up becoming very good at consuming. As

consumers of any goods, we look for products that work better for less cost. So, as a consumer in community, our expectations of others rise over time, and what we think the community should expect of us falls. That may be how consumers work, but it's not how community works. Over time, for example, people's irritating idiosyncrasies become clearer, and they're not quite as wonderful and supportive as they first seemed. At the same time, a community begins to ask more of an individual; for instance, in a church, you often are asked to be on a team or head up a committee. Soon, any given community, no matter how great it seemed at first, will seem to work less well and cost more—the exact opposite of what a good consumer wants.

Fortunately, there's something else we can practice instead. When you allow yourself to be seen and offer what you can contribute, you start looking suspiciously like a producer. Or to use the metaphor in John 15, you become one who "bears fruit," as well as enjoying the fruit *others* bear. Paul speaks of the "fruits of the Spirit": "love, joy, peace, patience, kindness, generosity, faithfulness, gentleness, and self-control" (Gal. 5:22–23). The good news is, you experience those even more when you contribute them to community (producing, "putting something in") than when you "get something out of it" (consuming). When you give love away, you feel the love within you even more strongly than when someone is giving love to you. When you focus more on giving and become a "producer," community satisfies a deeper longing.

Even more than being entertained or inspired or informed or even loved, human beings long for our unique identity to be acknowledged, our love to be requited, and our gifts to be received. If we remain consumers, we can't risk sharing ourselves enough for that to happen. And sharing ourselves is precisely what the treasure hunt invites us to do.

No one can do this for you

It can be a gift when someone cannot see or receive our best, because it forces us to see *ourselves* and to keep *ourselves* company; that's an essential skill for the treasure hunt. There are times when you have to forge ahead alone; that too is part of discerning community.

Our lives and callings are a curious mixture of solitude and community. This became clear to me at my ordination to pastoral ministry. The solitude struck me first. It felt like some sort of ritual test that asked a bigger question: Would I be able to withstand the solitude of ministry—keeping confidences, discerning decisions that could be unpopular, speaking God's word as it would (I hoped) be given to me in study and prayer? I felt that solitude in the ceremony's ritual and the church's architecture. I was the only person being ordained there that day, unlike in other churches in which people are often ordained in groups. I was ordained in the church where I grew up—not a large church but one with a long distance between the altar and the front row of pews. Several steps led up to the altar, and during the fifteen-minute rite of ordination, I knelt on one of those steps while the bishop stood on the top step. I found myself at his knee level. (At one point the bishop joked, during the rite's readings and prayers, "Are you still down there?")

I felt adrift in the seemingly infinite space between me and the rest of the church. I felt myself in a spiritual no-man's-land, all alone up there squeaking out my responses: "I will, and I ask God to help me." Where I was at that moment, only God could reach me. No one else could do for me what I was doing—taking a leap of faith that God had indeed called me to this holy madness, and I was indeed doing my best to answer. In many vocations, there are those moments. One jumps into the arms of Jesus and hopes.

Then I discovered a community behind me. Near the end of the ordination rite, the gathered clergy, all dressed up in their white robes in the front rows, come forward and lay hands on the person being ordained. Even greater than the community of clergy, however, is the community sitting behind them. Family, friends, church members from communities I'd been a part of, others who supported the ministry of the church—who would have guessed there were so many people willing to sit through an extra, ninety-minute church service on a Sunday afternoon? The community aspect didn't fully come home to me until a friend's ordination several years later. As one of the supporting clergy, I was charged with a reading. My heart broke to see my friend all alone, kneeling in front of the bishop in that spiritual no-man's-land. So with any prayerful power I had in the space of two lines, I sent him the message I had longed to hear when it had been my turn: You are not alone. We are with you. That was when I *really* knew that people had been doing that for me all along, even in the midst of that spiritual no-man's-land.

The paradox of intense solitude and community is not unique to ordained ministry. I experienced it again at my wedding several years later. What I thought was a quaint old-fashioned phrase about bridesmaids and groomsmen "standing up for you" is not quaint at all but very real. No one can do it for you, but marriage can definitely *not* be done by the couple alone. In other commitments, too, I have seen friends throw themselves on the grace of God alone and, paradoxically, rely on community at the same time—when they become a parent for the first time, or move to a new city, or start the job they've always wanted but aren't totally sure they're qualified for.

The psychologist Erik Erikson called this combination of solitude and community a creative tension between "isolation" and "intimacy."[8] Like many people, I spent a good portion of my young adulthood looking for intimacy, which for me meant "the man I'll spend the rest of my life with." It took a long time and some painful experiences to know that the only person I could count on spending the rest of my life with was me. But it is truly freeing to know, finally, that no one can do this journey for you, and sometimes not even *with* you. A relationship cannot be an end in itself; it is only a means to the end of knowing, loving, and being loved by God. *Then* another person or community can become traveling companions, or a home on the way, or a treasure for a time that could later provide a new clue. They could become people who can help you find, not "the one," but the One—God. Without such a grounding, we set ourselves up for turning clues into treasure and making idols out of relationships.

> *Clue:* Sometimes community shows up in person, but other times it's mainly in our head, where it still has a great effect on how we feel and act and think. In *Finding Your Own North Star*, Martha Beck encourages people to examine who their "everybody" is (as in, "*Everybody* thinks I'm smart/stupid")—and, if necessary, redefine "everybody" in a way that helps rather than hinders on the journey.[9] Who do you consider part of your "everybody"?

Leaving community

If a consumer perspective can't help us discern community, what other criteria are available? The answer for me came several months before I saw my marriage ending, in a class I was teaching called "Christian Foundations of Community." As we examined the theology and history of various intentional Christian communities, my students repeatedly asked me to define once and for all "what makes a good community." I told them that standards for community are difficult to define in black-and-white, just as it is difficult to tell when one is "on the right track" with the treasure hunt. As we saw with consolation and desolation, "it feels good" can lead one astray. Good feelings may be one sign that a community is working, but feelings can lead us astray when they're the *only* standard. But my students kept trying to pin me down, and finally, we all needed an anchor. So based on my study and experience of communities, I told them that three things are necessary for a good, healthy, life-giving community:

Individuals in the community are growing. "Growing" means individuals have the opportunity within community to become their best selves; they are healing, learning, using their gifts, loving and being loved, and becoming big enough for their lives; and there is nothing preventing them from following their treasure hunt.

The community is finding ways to accommodate that growth and change—which includes letting people leave, if they must.

The community discerns a shared *future* together; they are not joined merely by shared history, values, or interests.

When evaluating a community, it must be done with the knowledge that no community is perfect, or even *good* all the time. But sometimes the clues do point in the direction of the next "place." When that happens, it helps to have permission for two things: to let something end, and to hold onto the good. Both are necessary to balance out the natural human tendency to make things black-and-white.

When we let something end and move on, we avoid the dichotomy of "old equals good; new equals bad." Some relationships go deep rather than long; they seem to operate in *kairos* time rather than in *chronos*, to use the Greek biblical terms. Kairos is a time of opportunity, transformation, and sudden wholeness; as such, it is essentially timeless. For example, Paul writes to the Corinthians: "See, now is the acceptable time (kairos); see, now is the day of salvation!" (2 Corin. 6:2b). Kairos may last just a moment; it is a quality of time, not a quantity. Chronos, from which we get our term "chronological," is the measured time of hours, days, history—time with quantity. For example, in Matthew's story of Jesus' nativity, he recounts the visit of the wise men (the Magi) to the baby Jesus. "Then [King] Herod secretly called for the wise men and learned from them the exact time (chronos) when the star had appeared" (Matt. 2:7). When I think of kairos relationships, I think of friends from summer camp, teenage crushes, a best friend for an important but short season of life. The relationships may not last long, but they may have an effect far beyond their quantity, maybe even more than some chronos relationships: the people with whom we share our days and years, our work and our daily lives. Not all kairos relationships can exist in the chronos—and some may not be meant to in the first place.

When we hold onto the good, we avoid the trap of "old equals bad; new equals good." Sometimes the good in a past relationship is most obvious in terms of formation. In her novel *Prodigal Summer*, Barbara

Kingsolver writes of a young woman whose husband dies in an accident not long into a difficult marriage. Having moved from the city to her husband's family's farm, she found that her journey was changed forever when she accepted it as her own. Toward the end of the book, she reflects, "This marriage introduced me to myself." The marriage had been a remarkable clue to an unexpected treasure. I remembered that story when I first talked with Maggie and Brandon, the two college seniors who were debating where to move after graduation. Whether their relationship turned out to be clue or treasure, kairos or chronos, it just might introduce them to themselves.

When we leave any "place," we can be grateful for anything that has made us a bigger person. And if any place has provided sustenance as a "home on the way" and a treasure for a time, that's worth some gratitude, too, mixed with grief in leaving.

Grieving community

I have left or moved away from many communities, feeling the loss of some more than others. So far, the greatest loss has been the two-person community which dissolved when my marriage ended. The loss was so great that the feelings had to be parceled out in small chunks. The loss of our home together. The lost dream of having children together. The lost dream of growing old together. It was far too much to feel all at once. This too needs to be said about the treasure hunt: it can really, really hurt. Sometimes those wounds are a direct result of our choices. Often they are caused by a curve in the road we never could have seen coming.

When my husband and I separated, I needed a place to live, but even more than that, I needed shelter where I could recover and wait for new clues after this heartbreaking curve. I moved in with my parents, grateful for their hospitality. I was grateful especially for the particular room they offered: on the top floor of the house, its one window looked out on the twisted trunk of a great old oak tree. The leaves sheltered me, softening the light and turning my room into a protective treehouse. When the wind blew, one of the limbs brushed the house with friendly sighs. My cats sat on the desk and watched the birds and squirrels in its branches. Life and beauty continued, and that was good news.

Several weeks after moving in, I awoke from a sound sleep to a giant crash. Everyone in the house converged, trying to figure out where the car had crashed. In the dark, no one saw the tree. It wasn't until daybreak that we discovered it. The greatest part of the oak, an almost horizontal branch hanging all the way out over the road, had ripped away from the trunk, splitting the tree in half. Half was now lying in the road with its branches strewn everywhere, lifeless. The scene was straight out of a TV detective show—except that the dead body wasn't human, it was tree. But it felt like a death in the family all the same.

In the morning, the tree crew from the city treated me kindly when I went outside at the sound of their chainsaws, as they were efficiently clearing a path in the road. They said the kinds of things you say at funerals, with sorrowful faces and head-shaking: "It was a great tree." "It went too soon." I asked the sort of questions I would have posed to a doctor: "Why now? Was it somebody's fault? Should we have seen this coming?" I might have been asking similar questions about my marriage. Should I have seen this ending coming? Was I wrong about the clues that led me into the marriage, if the clues were now unavoidably leading me out of it? If it hurt this badly, did that mean it was the wrong thing to do? Ultimately, I couldn't answer those questions about my marriage any better than I could answer the questions about the tree.

In a strange way, mourning the tree was a relief. My internal grief had become external. Someone—or in this case, something—else knew how I felt: like a limb had been ripped off. That fallen tree meant something to me. Of course, grief doesn't have to have meaning or a message, but this one did. The meaning that emerged from the fallen tree made me wonder again about my own treasure hunt and whether I was somehow getting found. When the tree fell, there was no longer anything between my window and the full light of day. It transformed my hiding place into a place that light could reach. As uncomfortable and unwelcome as this transformation felt at the time, even that room became, literally, a place where I could be seen.

> *Clue:* Besides a fallen tree, many other images of grief are possible—an earthquake or tornado in one's life or psyche, for example. I think of Coventry Cathedral in England, which was bombed in World War II. The beautiful cathedral ruins, open to the sky, stand next to the new, modern cathedral. After a great loss, is there an area of your mind or heart that stands in ruins? Like the old Coventry Cathedral, could there be anything beautiful about it?

Further exploration

On choosing:

- In the film *Keeping the Faith*, a young Catholic priest has the opportunity to choose again his priestly vocation (or not) when he falls in love with an old friend (Spyglass Entertainment, 2000).
- Barry Schwartz writes provocatively about choices from the perspective of social science in *The Paradox of Choice: Why More Is Less*. While he primarily addresses consumer goods rather than intangibles such as community, many of his conclusions apply to the latter, too (New York: HarperCollins, 2004).

On being seen in community:

- The film *The Full Monty* tells the story of a group of discouraged men wrestling with being literally, fully "seen"—and more metaphorically, having their value recognized as well (Redwave Films, 1997).
- *Lying Awake*, a novel by Mark Salzman, portrays a nun with extraordinary gifts, which lead to difficult choices in community (New York: Vintage Contemporaries, 2000).

- In the film *Coach Carter,* a basketball coach inspires his team to academic as well as athletic prowess. Like similar stories of a committed adult facing an uphill battle in an inner-city school, it's a great example of people rising to the challenge of the way they are seen. *Coach Carter* also contains a great scene in which one of the players quotes the entire Marianne Williamson passage excerpted in this chapter (Paramount Pictures, 2005).

On healthy community:

I used these classic texts on community in my class, and they helped us talk about what makes a "good" community.
- *The Rule of Benedict: Insights for the Ages,* by Joan Chittister, O.S.B. (New York: Crossroad, 1992).
- *Community and Growth,* by Jean Vanier, rev. ed. (New York and Mahwah, NJ: Paulist Press, 1989)

NINE

Treasure Hunting You

Where your treasure is, there your heart will be also.
—Jesus (Matthew 6:21)
Wherever your heart is, there you will find your treasure.
—Paulo Coelho[1]

WE NEED A COMMUNITY of people who not only look *at* us but also look *for* us. We need people to help us see ourselves, often because our treasure is buried so deep. And we need people to remind us that other forces are at work besides our own digging and hard work.

Clues to myself

While working at Santa Clara University I received a random email one day that named my childhood address in suburban Michigan and inquired whether I had lived there. I had indeed, but my family had moved twenty-five years earlier. I assumed this information had been unearthed on the Internet somewhere, so I was astonished and a little freaked out. I was also intrigued, so I wrote back, politely, "Who wants to know?" The reply was even more astonishing: "We live there now. We just dug up the dogwood tree, and if you used to live there, you'll know what we found."

The email had a supernatural quality, as if I were being contacted from the twilight zone. Maybe I was—except that the "past life" making contact was still *my* life. Yes, I did know what was under that dogwood tree. No, it wasn't a clue to an unsolved murder or something else that would make good TV. It was buried treasure.

I had just turned seven when my family moved from that house to California. As a way to say good-bye to the house and my Michigan life, I filled a baby-food jar with "treasure" and buried it in the courtyard outside the front door, under the dogwood tree. I included a note with my name and my new address.

Thus began a brief correspondence with the woman who now lives in my childhood home. I first pictured her as my mother's age, but I realize now that she is probably much closer to my own. Her two young girls have the same rooms my sister and I did—the older daughter has the very room where I myself had learned to be an older sister. The woman sent pictures of her daughters, and I sent a picture of myself burying the treasure.

The correspondence culminated with the arrival of a package: the treasure itself, which had found me at last. I'd had several weeks to imagine what it would mean to me. I wanted it to answer questions I had about myself as a child and about what I had valued before I grew up and got confused by what I thought I was *supposed* to value. I wanted it to be a clue to the unsolved mysteries of myself. I hoped it would tell me whether I was on the right track.

With such great expectations, opening the box was a disappointment. What I considered "treasure" as a seven-year-old included several unidentifiable objects I had made out of bread dough, a drawing of a clown, a picture of myself, a jack, a penny. Most poignant to me was the note I wrote: "I used to live here." That move was my first big leave-taking, and even though I hadn't left yet, I was practicing the past tense. I had no idea how to feel, much less express, my sadness about moving. I left a part of me in that home that I had loved with all my heart, and I buried treasure there to prove it—because where your treasure is, there your heart will be.

I couldn't have explained my thoughts or feelings at the time. Burying them was the best I could do. But nothing important will stay buried forever.

Hiding

All of us live with various kinds of brokenness that cause us to bury all kinds of things, from memories to talents to personality traits. Most of us have deep, unknown possibilities within us. That's why we need a community with eyes for the possible, who can see beyond the everyday mask we show to others. On the surface, perhaps we are pretending to be good at something in order to keep a job. Perhaps we are pretending to be bad at something in order to avoid responsibility. Maybe we are so confused that we are just making up a self as we go along, not sure *who* we are today and if we will want to be that person tomorrow.

In *Let Your Life Speak*, Parker Palmer quotes a poem by May Sarton in which the poet has "worn other people's faces."[2] Sometimes our masks aren't truly *others'* faces; they are versions of our own. They may come from our past, as we try to appear as hip and young and smart as we once were. Or they may come from our future, the way we'd like to be eventually. Those masks proclaim that someday we will be more spiritual, more fun, less neurotic, more cultured, more organized, or less self-centered. Even if we never become that self we imagine, we can wear the mask, strenuously hoping that if we can convince other people that's who we are, we may yet convince ourselves.

Throughout my twenties, my costume for Halloween parties was "my shadow side," inspired by the psychology and self-help books I'd been reading. I loved that mask, not only because it was easy to put together—black clothes with black and white face paint, topped with a colorful scarf as the "creative streak"—but also because I imagined it to be unique, with some humor and sophistication thrown in. Perhaps *that* was my true mask: one day I would be more unique, humorous, and sophisticated than I actually felt.

At times masks can be helpful; since we tend to become what we practice, "acting as if" we are a certain way can form our character. (Is it possible that I *have* become more humorous and sophisticated over time?) On the other hand, sometimes we don't even want to *be* that self we imagine; we just want to be *seen* that way. So we wear the mask and live with the fear that we'll get found out as an impostor.

That fear can be exhausting, but it may be better than the alternative: far better to have a mask rejected, we reason, than the real self behind it. That strategy carries a high price: with masks on, we give up the possibility of true intimacy—not only with others but with ourselves and with God. Judeo-Christian tradition says that human beings are made in the image of God—"fearfully and wonderfully made," says Psalm 139:14. When we wear a mask of any kind, we live a distorted image of *ourselves* and thereby separate ourselves from the One who made us.

The real question, though, isn't whether a particular mask is helpful or harmful. The real question is what we lose by hiding. What's behind the mask that's not allowed to shine? When the mask comes off, we may discover that the person underneath is just who we always wanted to be. But if we masquerade as our imaginary former or future self, or hide behind the personality or talents of someone else entirely, how can we or anyone else appreciate who we are today, with our God-given talents and personality? How will we ever learn that those are good enough, and even wonderful? How will we ever find that treasure buried deep within?

And where will we find the energy to keep digging?

> **Clue:** In Matthew 25:14–30, Jesus tells the story of three servants asked to steward different amounts of their master's money while he is away. One servant, given the smallest measure, hides his portion in the ground instead of investing it like the other two. What might he be afraid of? Can you relate?

An alternative to hard work

When I talk about the treasure hunt with Lutheran pastors, teachers, or academics, they sometimes express a concern that I am focusing too much on what we do—our "works." They are suspicious of this emphasis on our seeking, our choices, and our desires, which they interpret either as a burden or as an inappropriate focus on the self. For example, here is Douglas Schuurman, the author of Vocation: Discerning Our Callings in Life: "We need to recover the sense that our lives are in many ways 'given' to us by forces beyond our control but ultimately in the loving hands of a provident God."[3] It's not about what we do, they say. It's all about what God does for us.

I agree: We don't find God because we seek God. We are enabled to seek God because God has already found us. So what's all this digging and seeking and journeying that sounds like hard work? They are our response to the clues we receive from God's grace. They are the actions that allow our lives to take shape according to God's grace to us. They're the way we begin to come out of hiding.

As I share treasure hunt stories of my own and those of students I've worked with, one word keeps repeating itself: "let."

- *Let* God speak, both within you and through other people and circumstances. Don't rule out either source of insight.
- *Let* God be God. You don't have to "see around corners," anticipating consequences that can't possibly be predicted.
- *Let* go of your plans when they interfere with God's plans for you.
- *Let* the treasure find you, even if it takes twenty-five years or more.

One time a student noticed all these "lets" and commented that such language contradicts what he hears most of the time. Others usually advise him, "Make sure you get good grades, graduate from college, and get a good job with health insurance." Work hard and make it happen, he's been told repeatedly. So, he wanted to know, what's all this about "letting" it happen? I understood where he was coming from. I remember my early twenties, too, when everyone I encountered simply *overflowed* with suggestions for ways to "make it happen" with a career and financial security. The implication was that without those, my life would never turn out well.

Behind that implication was the fear of the worst: what if my life totally fell apart? (There's that arrogance again; "making it happen" doesn't make us immune to falling apart any more than good discernment does.)

Mixed with that fear was functional atheism and the assumption that no one would have a hand in my future except myself. The language of "letting" comes from different assumptions entirely. It assumes that, in fact, there *is* Someone who has a hand in my future. Instead of fear, it implies a faith in this One who can see around corners where we cannot and who provides the company, resources, and clues we need along the way.

A purpose looking for its person

While we're busy trying to "make" our callings happen, other forces are at work. People call those forces God or Spirit, "serendipity" or "fate," or "the universe." However it is described, when a person and his or her calling connect, it's not always clear who has been looking for whom. Often it seems like the opposite of the usual remark, "Now there's a person who has found her purpose." What if, instead, there's a *purpose* who has found its *person*? What if there's something else going on in the treasure hunt besides our own discovering and following clues? What if the treasure is somehow looking for us too?

Remember the golfer Rannulph Junuh, looking for his own authentic shot in *The Legend of Bagger Vance*? He is working so hard trying to make it happen, but the harder he works and worries and sweats, the further he seems to get from his goal. In the midst of that pressure, his caddy and spiritual guide, Bagger Vance, has good news: "There's a perfect shot out there looking for each one of us. All we have to do is get ourselves out of the way."

That sounds simple enough: "all" we have to do is get our anxieties, stubbornness, blindness, and mistaken convictions out of the way. "All" we have to do is keep taking the next best step and letting things unfold. Easier said than done, that takes patience and self-awareness and a willingness to experiment and make mistakes. It turns out that *letting* things happen might actually be more work than *making* them happen—but a different kind of work. Still, the language of "letting" is much more true to how vocation works, just as Bagger says. Literature, history, and personal anecdotes offer myriad examples of people who say they didn't find their calling—somehow, *it* found them.

If the treasure really is looking for us, then the hard work we do is mainly "getting ourselves out of the way." The opposite is easy to do; for example, we let our fear get in the way of seizing a great opportunity. Or we get convinced (by others or ourselves) that we only make poor decisions, so it becomes difficult to make a good one. As my students pointed out, the culture will urge you to work hard to make it happen. If we are to get out of our own way and let our calling find us, then we need an alternative language, and people with whom to practice it.

Practicing the language of faith

Plenty of people would be happy to help us become fluent in fear, which wakes us up at night to worry over a job interview or a first date or a potential move. But where do we learn the language of faith and get conversational practice? How do we recognize a Bagger Vance, who reminds us that the treasure is seeking us, too?

I know plenty of people who want to have success and financial security and health insurance (I count myself among them). And yet some also have a sense that they are not the only ones deciding our choices. We can be bilingual, so to speak: we attend to normal human concerns, but we also encourage each other to have faith in a God who does not abandon us to our own choices, anxieties, and blindness. It can be hard to find this kind of conversation partner, though. It's as if people fear that if they become fluent in the language of "letting," they or their loved ones will stop acting on their own behalf.

But that's not how the language of faith works. In fact, we do plenty of "acting" in this seeking and digging for buried treasure. With our best spiritual disciplines and life skills, we attend to clues, try out roles, participate in communities of discernment, and share our gifts whenever we can and see what happens. But we sell God (and ourselves) short when

> *Clue:* Educators are often good at "looking for" people. The root word of education, *educare*, means "drawing out"—not "putting in," as is commonly practiced.[5] What treasure has been or might be "drawn out" of you through education?

we think we are on our own to find the treasure. We also sell ourselves (and God) short when we sit back and wait for life to come to us. On this treasure hunt, the saying goes, we "work as if everything depends on us, and pray as if everything depends on God."[4] It's not a question of either-or. For the fullest life of possibility, we have to do both.

Actually, we get to do both. In God's infinite love and mercy, God allows us the privilege of participating in our own lives—not only to "guess the plan," but to shape it through our seeking and finding. But here too, as always, God goes first: God teaches us to seek by seeking us.

The quintessential seeker

We have a God who comes to look for us. In the incarnation, God came to Earth as Jesus, Emmanuel, meaning "God is with us" (Matt.1:23). Why did he come? "To seek out and to save the lost" (Luke 19:10). Throughout the gospels we see Jesus' ministry as the hunt for one treasure or another—a tax collector here, a blind man there. He tells stories of finding lost sheep, lost coins, a lost son (Luke 15:1–32).

Jesus' ministry of seeking does not end with his death. John's gospel tells the story of Easter morning as another search: the search for Mary Magdalene, who is truly lost after Jesus' death (John 20:1–18). The story begins with Mary Magdalene visiting Jesus' tomb—certain, I imagine, that after her Lord's death, she would never be happy again. The gospels tell of Mary and some other women going to the tomb to anoint Jesus' body. I imagine them as being glad to have something to do and grateful for a reason to be with him. Perhaps they felt closer to him there. But then Mary and the others find the tomb empty, the body gone. Mary is devastated, robbed of the body and thus of the last small comfort she was holding onto.

With this new loss on top of the great loss, she keeps seeking. She finds the gardener and begs him to tell her where the body is. And then the "gardener" calls her name, and she recognizes him as Jesus. He tells her, in effect, that she's not supposed to be in a graveyard holding onto him—she's supposed to be out in the world continuing on the great adventure to which he had called her and the others.

I had never understood this part of the story: Why does Jesus, on the first morning of his resurrected life, show up in a *graveyard*, of all places? He could have gone anywhere, done anything. Had it been me, I think I would have climbed a mountain or at least eaten a really good breakfast. Instead, Jesus returned to the place of death and decay from which he

> *Clue:* Having experienced the death of a special person, a relationship, or a dream, plenty of us would relate to Mary Magdalene's certainty of being lost forever. When have you been lost in such a way? How were you looked for, or found?

had just been freed. It seems like the *last* place he would want to return.

Except for this: He knew Mary would be there. He must have come to look for her.

This story makes me want to trust Jesus. I want to trust that he is always coming to look for me, even when I feel like Mary Magdalene— hanging out in places of death and loss, mucking around in my own compost, trying to hold on instead of letting go. I want to trust that if that's where Jesus showed up on the very first morning of his new life, he shows up there still, coming to look for us wherever we are and however we are hiding.

Being sought

Even as God is seeking us, we get to participate. In "working as if everything depends on us," we help ourselves get found. Using our gifts, practicing generosity, following clues—every small attempt on our part to come out of hiding contributes to possibility. In short, we *find* our vocation by *living* our vocation the best we can.

The film *August Rush* dramatizes this spiritual, time-consuming, and sometimes grueling process.[6] We first meet the young Evan in an orphanage, a boy with extraordinary musical gifts. He is impassioned by the conviction that eventually his unknown parents will hear his music and recognize him at last. In his quest to get his music heard as widely as possible, Evan encounters clues along the way. On the streets of New York City, he meets Wizard, who encourages him to choose a stage name. To help him consider his new identity, he asks Evan, "What do you most want to be?" "Found," he replies. Wherever he goes, Evan puts his heart—in the form of music—into helping himself get found by the parents he's never met. His extraordinary gifts are matched by a remarkable faith that music will bring him together with the treasure he craves: family.

Being found

As the One who created us, God knows better than anyone what treasure is hidden behind our masks and what a treasure we are. Even when we don't seem to be finding anything whatsoever of value, God and the treasure are on their way to us. Sometimes, we are surprised by the almost absurd ways we are found—such as receiving buried treasure in the mail, twenty-five years later. Unlike Evan, I hadn't even known I was looking for it, but I'm so glad it found me. To me, that's what God is like—someone who finds us, sometimes when we don't even know we're looking.

I am also grateful for the woman who stewarded my treasure so carefully and helped it find its way back to me. After twenty-five years of dampness, the smell alone would have destined the jar for the trash in many households. It makes me wonder if there are even more people in the world who, knowingly or not, hold our intangible treasures in trust until it is time for the treasures to return to us. Perhaps this is one of the gifts of communities of discernment, a gift which isn't realized until years later. I think of people who saw things in me years and years before I could see them myself.

Even before my buried treasure arrived, stories like this had always captivated me—stories about a letter in a bottle washed up on shore, or a package which reaches its destination despite many perils and delays along the way. The messages seem to take on a life of their own, as if the universe has somehow taken charge of getting them where they need to

> **Clue:** To August Rush, "treasure" means family, but in other stories, it means a romantic partner or a place to belong. Like him, we each have our own "treasure" we seek, as well as our own "music"—ways we put our heart out there and help ourselves get found. What are yours?

go—like a purpose which seeks its person. Or like the music in *August Rush*, which takes on a life of its own to draw Evan's parents to him even though they hadn't known he was alive. They had not, in fact, been looking for him—but through music, treasure found them all.

I didn't consciously know any of this when I buried that jar of treasure so many years ago. But receiving it back so many years later gives me yet another reason to believe that the universe can be trusted—even with my greatest treasures.

Just what God always wanted

The more we journey—the more clues we follow, the more treasure we discover—the harder it becomes to say *who* exactly is digging, seeking, and finding, and *what* exactly the treasure is. Is it ourselves, God, or something else, or all of the above at different times? A spiritual director told me once that the treasure I was finding was my self. And yet it seems to be more than that, and also less. At times it seems like the treasure is no less than God. Other times I believe the treasure is not so much finding my self, but rather finding vocation, a place where my self can belong and be known. Part of the journey may indeed be figuring out what kind of journey it is, but all these slippery boundaries make it difficult to say precisely. The journey is easier to narrate *particularly* than to explain *generally*; it is better described than defined.

Paulo Coelho narrates such a journey powerfully and imaginatively in his novel, *The Alchemist*, in which finding treasure is a kind of homecoming after a long journey. Many of us may experience such a homecoming more than once, as one treasure becomes a clue to the next. We are always seeking and finding, and using our clues and treasures not only for our own sake but for others'. We come home to ourselves when we begin to realize that our calling is how we love—love that we don't generate ourselves but that moves into and through us from God. When we practice our skills of seeking, we can't help but become closer to God in a kind of homecoming. After all, our loving and longing and seeking are the things we have most in common with God, because God loves and longs and seeks for us.

God's love is not a passive "warm fuzzy" that waits for us to arrive. God's love is a passionate, active force, which pursues and accompanies and envelops us when we least expect it. God sees the best in us and never stops pursuing us, even when we keep stumbling over our own feet and can't imagine what we're looking for or why. Simply put, God delights in us. Earlier in this book we saw how God's Wisdom has always delighted in us ever since the beginning (Prov. 8:30-31). God delights in us even while our best is still hidden. As we travel, we can bask in that knowledge that we are loved and sought. As Anthony de Mello writes: "Behold God beholding you ... and smiling."[7]

We may start out seeking *our* passion, but we will end up finding *God's* passion, and we will discover that God has a passion for us. We might think of God placing gifts within us—similar to the biblical perspective of being created in the image of God. Then God never stops looking for those gifts in us and drawing them out so that they can be used in the world. In this process God reveals us to ourselves. Through everything we do and all we become, God draws us to himself—and to ourselves. Even when our selves or our lives are not what we want them to be, *even then*, we are just what God always wanted. God is *that* passionate about us—passionate enough to keep seeking us, drawing us out, and calling us home.

> *Clue:* Shel Silverstein's book, *The Missing Piece*,[8] has a wonderful image of a shape looking for its missing piece. If you could imagine yourself as God's "missing piece," a shape God needs to fill some kind of hole somewhere, what shape would you be? How does God treasure the shape you are?

Further exploration

On hiding:

- The song "Undiscovered," by James Morrison, invites hearers to consider the difference between "hiding" and being "not yet found" (*Undiscovered*, Universal, 2006).
- *Owning Your Own Shadow: Understanding the Dark Side of the Psyche*, by Robert A. Johnson, may have been the first inspiration for my "shadow side" costume. He draws on Jungian archetypes in his discussion of "the gold in the shadow," which can be as difficult to "own" as the shadow itself. He writes: "It is more disrupting to find that you have a profound nobility of character than to find out you are a bum. Of course you are both ..." (San Francisco: HarperSanFrancisco, 1991), 8.

On coming full circle:

- "Love After Love," a poem by Derek Walcott, reminds me of Marion Woodman's line, " ... one day you will recognize yourself coming down the road to meet yourself ..." You can find it in *Ten Poems to Change Your Life*, by Roger Housden (New York: Harmony Books, 2001, 95).
- Elizabeth Gilbert tells a story near the end of *Eat Pray Love* which reminds me of these other examples of coming full circle. (New York: Penguin Books, 2006).
- In the tearjerker film *P.S. I Love You*, a young widow receives letters written to her by her late husband and finds in them clues to who she had been when they met (Alcon Entertainment, 2007).

On a "purpose" (or something else) with a life of its own:

- In the film *Message in a Bottle*, a woman tracks down the author of a message she finds washed up on the beach (Bel Air Entertainment, 1999).

- After a plane crash lands him on a deserted island, the main character of the film *Cast Away* shows extraordinary commitment to a FedEx package that survived the crash with him (DreamWorks, 2000).

TEN

God's Passion for Us

*How long the road is. But, for all the time the journey
has already taken, how you have needed every
second of it in order to learn what the road passes by.*
—Dag Hammarskjöld[1]

LOOKING BACK ON MY YOUNG-ADULT JOURNEY, I realize that as
many times as I wondered if I was doing it "right," that wasn't the real
question after all. The real question was, *"Will I be okay?"* "Okay" encom-
passed a variety of things: safe, successful, loved. I was simply anxious
about how my life would turn out. This wondering takes on a particular
urgency in students nearing graduation. There is usually much guessing,
for example, in dating relationships: Are we going to "end up" together
or not? Or, is my career going to "turn out" well? Am I going to "end up"
living in this city? Where will I ultimately find the treasure? And finally,
when will I be done searching? We want to know the answer to a funda-
mental question: Am I *ever* going to live happily ever after?

> *Clue:* About what are you currently asking your-
> self, "How will it turn out"? What milestone or
> "end" are you anticipating?

No guarantees

Not only at graduation times but often I've asked similar questions about relationships and career. When I was dating the man I eventually married, I wanted to skip to the ending and find out how it all turned out. But at what "ending" do you know that something has "turned out"? We never know, and as soon as we think we do, we might find that while the event or relationship has ended, the memories and the meaning continue to change. For example, perhaps a certain relationship is better as kairos than chronos—who can say for sure? We know that individuals "end up" dying, but we don't usually say that "dead" is how someone's life *turns out*. Instead, we look at things like meaning and love and connection, and even then we really can't measure an outcome precisely.

Discernment both requires and produces a large amount of humility, which teaches us that we can't make decisions based on how something will turn out in the final analysis—because we never know enough to declare it "final." Some people learn this through day-to-day struggles with chronic illness or addiction, where any "outcome" is too difficult to measure or define or even consider, and so there is only "one day at a time."

For someone like me who grew up with fairy tales and adventure stories with lots of happily-ever-afters, this can be a grim realization: there are no guarantees about how one's life will "turn out." In our real-life stories, we cannot be assured that the hero will triumph. We do not know that the romance will last after riding off into the sunset. We can't count on physical or mental health. We can't rest in the knowledge that this one (person, job, home) is *finally* the end of the road, the once-and-for-all treasure we had been seeking. As fragile human beings, we do not have impervious armor or foolproof solutions, and there are no guarantees that we won't get seriously hurt on this treasure hunt.

Anxiety and trust

As treasure hunters, we have staked our lives, or at least our happiness and well-being, on this journey. But with no guarantees, what *can* we count on? Where, besides denial, can we find some relief from the anxiety and insecurity this creates? What or whom can we trust, and how?

I hear people talk about the importance of trusting God on the spiritual journey, as if trust were a prerequisite for getting anywhere. It is not so hard to trust God when we believe common myths: that God ensures happy endings and that God wouldn't let anything hurt us too badly along the way. "God never gives us more than we can handle," some say. It is much harder to trust God when our journey reveals the truths that some stories do not end happily, that some paths wound painfully or even mortally, that we can become completely overwhelmed by much more than we can "handle." Making the journey means learning to keep the faith despite losses and disappointments and to trust the way even when no one and nothing else seems trustworthy.

Trust in something or Someone offers the only antidote to the anxiety that accompanies a lack of guarantees. I hesitated to tell my students that because I was afraid that they would *try* even harder to trust. And they were already trying so hard to do the right thing and make their parents and professors proud. I wanted to remove burdens, not add one—especially a tall order like trust. I was afraid that if I told them to "just trust God," I would be adding insult to injury, or giving a diagnosis without a cure: "No wonder you're anxious—you don't trust well enough." It's about as helpful to tell an anxious person, "Just trust God," as it is to tell an obsessed person, "Just don't think about it."

A different approach to trust is offered in 1 Corinthians 13. It's a text often heard as instructions: "Love is patient, love is kind. It does not envy, it does not boast, it is not proud" (v. 4, NIV). Read as a wedding text, it has sounded to me like an instruction list at which we should try harder: "For a good marriage, do this *or else.*" Later in that same text, it reads: "Love always trusts." I was suspicious at first: so now I have to try harder at trusting in order to *love*? A tall order indeed.

But then I read it again: "It (love) always protects, always trusts, always hopes, always perseveres" (v. 7). *Always* is clearly beyond human capabilities, but it is not beyond the capacity of God's love. What if "having love" means being *filled* with Love rather than trying to *do* love?

What if love and trust and all the other things Love brings are gifts and not just human efforts?

Like 1 John 4:18, which promises, "Perfect love casts out fear," 1 Corinthians 13 invites Love to come in and take over our lives—to rearrange the furniture, clean out the closets, and scrub the windows clean. In the process of moving in and filling us more and more, Love leaves less and less room for fear. Love enables and inspires us to trust and protect and hope and persevere. When we are impatient or unkind, envious or proud—or, for that matter, anxious—what we lack is *love*, not morality or ability or effort.

When God's love fills us and enables us to trust, we can rest from our fears and anxiety. We make space for that love through all kinds of practices that are far easier than "just trusting": being of service to others, taking quiet time in prayer and reflection, and doing whatever we need to do next, with attentiveness despite our anxiety. Yes, the journey is smoother if we trust the way. But the journey doesn't *require* trust as much as it *creates* it. When we practice those things, Love creeps in. We might find ourselves trusting before we even know what happened. Love is *that* powerful.

We have an important choice to make, which affects how we experience the journey, even if it doesn't affect how life "turns out." One option: We can tell the story of our journey as the story of wounds, losses, and disappointments—treasures that turned out not to be "the one," dead ends where a clue didn't pan out, or our failure to find anything worthwhile in our search. Any of us, if we live long enough, can find plenty of evidence for how we have been damaged by the journey, even irreparably. The second option may be harder, but it is infinitely worthwhile: We can look for evidence of love instead, since Love fills us, even in spite of ourselves.

> *Clue:* We don't always "make space" for God's love, but sometimes God shows up despite us. Look at John 20:19 (NIV): "When the disciples were together, with the doors locked for fear of the Jews, Jesus came and stood among them and said, 'Peace be with you!' " How do you tend to "lock the doors," and how does Love break in?

A love story

The Bible is full of people with a past, people who have been damaged by life and its losses. One of them is "the woman at the well," as she is often called—the Samaritan woman whom Jesus meets in John 4. Jesus knows her painful story, she discovers. After a conversation about water, and the living water he offers, Jesus seems to bait her: " 'Go, call your husband and come back.' The woman answered him, 'I have no husband'" (vv. 16–17). Then, Jesus reveals what he knows about her journey: "Jesus said to her, 'You are right in saying, "I have no husband"; for you have had five husbands, and the one you have now is not your husband. What you have said is true!' " (vv. 17–18). This could have been gossip and judgment—*five* husbands?!—but based on what comes next, it clearly wasn't.

A few verses later, the woman says, " 'I know that Messiah is coming' (who is called Christ). 'When he comes, he will proclaim all things to us.' Jesus said to her, 'I am he, the one who is speaking to you' " (vv. 25–26). Could it be that what Jesus had proclaimed to her was not only the source of living water and the place of true spiritual worship but also the truth of her own story and her own worthiness? Whatever it was, the news must be shared:

> Then the woman left her water jar and went back to the city. She said to the people, "Come and see a man who told me everything I have ever done! He cannot be the Messiah, can he?" ... Many Samaritans from that city believed in him because of the woman's testimony, "He told me everything I have ever done" (vv. 28–29, 39).

Had Jesus simply recited the facts of her history, I doubt it would have made such an impact. I believe it was the *way* he told her story, the way he interpreted it to her, and the love with which he saw her and her difficult history. We aren't privy to that telling in her life, but we could consider how Jesus might tell *our* story as a love story.

God teaches us to love by loving us. God teaches us to seek by seeking us. God draws us close and holds on so that we can let go. We may start out seeking our passion, but we will end up finding God's passion, and we will discover that God's passion is us. If part of the journey is figuring out what kind of journey it is, then here is a potential description: The journey of seeking our calling appears to be a love story. That's how God tells our story.

> **Clue:** In *The Awakened Heart*, Gerald May writes, "Instead of trying to know what love is by abstract concepts and definitions, I suggest you seek a more direct appreciation of your own experiences of love. You might think of it as telling your story of love.... What is your experience of love right now? How do you sense yourself loving, being loved, being in love?" [2]

Looking for love

When we are looking for evidence of love, it is tempting to focus first on who loves or has loved us. As a spiritual director for young adults, I often ask them where they are experiencing God's presence in their lives. They frequently responded, "I experience God in the people who love me." I sometimes say the same thing myself, but seeing life this way is problematic. When we don't have the companionship we are seeking, or when those companions are not loving us the "right" way, we feel abandoned not only by people but by God.

No matter where we're looking for love, it seldom comes in the form we expect. People love us the way *they* want to, not the way *we* want them to. We saw this in discerning community: If we depend on certain individuals for our "supply" of love, we are bound to be disappointed at some times, and we will feel insecure at many times. I knew this disappointment and insecurity well during a lonely time of my life. I was several years out of college, and I wanted a boyfriend, a partner, a companion who would love me the way I *wanted* to be loved.

I had just moved to Cambridge, and I found a position as a part-time nanny to support myself in graduate school. On weekdays, I cared for the two children, ages four and seven, for several hours in the evenings. We would play games or read books or visit the park across the street, and then I would make dinner. On weekends we'd go on outings in the city. As many people do when they become parents or work with children, I developed new capacities: the ability to cook daily meals, to cut tiny fingernails, to love a screaming child. I loved those kids, but I still would have said that I felt abandoned by God in relationships. I defined love as a certain kind of relationship that supplied the love I needed, and when I looked at my life, I found that unbearably lacking.

Years later, I thought I had solved the loneliness problem by getting married. But during that first year of marriage, I still found myself lonely at times when my husband didn't love me "right." When I wanted love in the form of washing dishes, I would get nice words. When I wanted love in nice words, I would get love in fixing the computer. He showed me love in his own way, and it didn't always match the love I wanted him to supply.

On a retreat during that time, it finally hit me: if I could somehow find God in my capacity to love my husband, rather than focusing on getting my husband to love me differently, I would be a lot less disappointed and a lot more secure. This made sense when I looked back to my year of being a nanny. The most wonderful thing about that year was the capacities it brought out in me. Those kids introduced me to this amazingly patient, fun, creative, problem-solving woman. (And who knew I could even cook?!) They went way beyond any qualities I could have conjured up on my own—I could only attribute them to God's love acting in and through me. Many times since, that's where I have found evidence of love: in my own capacity to love. That's a place that God continues to find me, in my love for people or for a cause or even for my cats.

Rather than wondering how something will turn out and guessing at the ending, we look for evidence of love along the way instead. This can be helpful not only for telling the story of the past but also for discerning where the story might go next. You might ask yourself: "What service is being given and received? What is being learned? How is the relationship or job or study helping me grow into the person I was created to be?" When the outcome cannot be foreseen or measured, there is tremendous freedom to make the best decisions today based on *those* questions, instead of on "How will it all turn out?"

It helps to tell your love story in a way that respects your own skills of seeking, which can be another source of trust. When I bought my first home, my anxious mind went straight to catastrophe. I worried that I would lose it somehow—perhaps through financial trouble or a job change. I was certain I would never find another home quite as nice, because this was such a fluke; in the seamless way that the clues unfolded, it was as if God had said, "Here—have a house." But then I realized there was another way to understand the story, which better appreciated my own skills of seeking. I had done the work to find this house. I had learned how to get a mortgage, worked with a real estate agent, analyzed inspection reports, and made the decision to buy a beautiful place. I had gotten myself and two cats moved, and I had furnished and decorated our new home. I certainly did not do all that alone, and I asked for help a lot along the way. But if this house turns out not to be "the one" forever (which is most likely), I will still have those skills. When I tell this particular love story, my anxiety subsides when I remember to include myself as an active love-er, not just a passive recipient. As with all skills of discernment, these skills will be there the next time I need them, and they improve with practice.

> *Clue:* The Prayer of Saint Francis asks, "Grant that I may not so much seek to be consoled as to console; to be understood as to understand; to be loved as to love." How might this help you focus on developing your capacities for love, rather than looking for love from someone else?

A big enough dream

Skills of loving and discerning are signs of God's love in us, but the love we "contain" is not the only love at work. God's infinite love contains us: "In him (God) we live and move and have our being" (Acts 17:28). No matter where our journeys take us, we live and move within God's dreams for us. We can find the general aspects of these dreams in the Bible: eternal life, knowing God, the fruits of the Spirit. But there are specific dreams too. Those are the dreams we seek when we look for our passion.

Sometimes people get in sync with God's dream for them early in life, like my friends who farm sixty-seven acres just south of Minneapolis. They aren't just growing organic food to feed their family. They are growing a dream of living sustainably as the world's fossil fuel supply shrinks. Their connection to their neighbors, integration in the local economy, and knowledge of organic methods are truly revelatory to someone like me whose meat is usually purchased in plastic and whose car is like an extra limb. When I visit them, I watch wistfully as their young boys grow up outdoors—picking berries, caring for chickens, and shucking peas from the garden.

When I was married, periodically my husband and I would visit these farming friends together. He and I used to talk about—idolized, even—the way they were living their dream. In their thirties, already they are living a life guided by their values in a way many people never achieve in an entire lifetime. Those visits inspired my husband and me to dream our own dreams and examine how we were living our own values. A more recent visit of mine had the same effect—except now it was just *me* and *my* dreams and *my* values. That dream of "ours" ended when the marriage did.

Perhaps that's why I noticed some different things about my friends' dreams on the latest visit. I noticed, for example, that money can be tight when you're supporting a family on a small farm, even when you've inherited the land. I noticed the setbacks caused by weather (such as significant losses in a recent planting of hazelnut seedlings) and changes in the local economy. I noticed the sacrifices in time and energy, and sometimes in other dreams that fell by the wayside. I noticed that there is no guarantee for how *any* of this will all turn out. Through all this, my friends have remarkable energy—when one thing doesn't work (like the seedlings), they're ready to try the next thing. They take the frequent discouragement in stride because they understand something about dreams that I'd never grasped: A dream worth dreaming occupies your energy and love and passion not just for months or years but for a lifetime. It's not *supposed* to be perfect, or guaranteed, or ever "done."

In the book *Big Questions, Worthy Dreams*, Sharon Daloz Parks calls this a "big enough dream," a dream with a capital D.[3] This is the kind of dream that you don't "possess"—*it* possesses *you*. The dream of this farm and the way of life it supports—that dream lives through my friends, rather than vice versa. We don't dream our biggest dreams at all—our dreams dream us. This is a dream bigger than anything we ourselves can "handle." But if the dream is big enough, it doesn't have to be *completed* to give us great joy and satisfaction. If the dream is big enough to have a life of its own, even significant setbacks are not enough to defeat it.

So what do we do with dreams that appear defeated? It helps to look for the Dream behind the dream—what some might call a "vision" for an individual or community. For example, my friends keep focused on their values and way of life, without spending too much regret on an individual failed planting. In my own life, behind my failed marriage was a dream of friendship, partnership, and community. Visiting my friends, I could see that that dream is alive and well, despite the end of that particular relationship. I see that like my friends' farm, this is still a dream worth a lifetime of energy and love, even through setbacks and losses.

Shortly before the most recent farm trip, I watched *Babette's Feast*, a tale of love and longing and regret.[4] In the movie, General Lowenhielm as a young man falls in love with Martina. Since he cannot have her love, he pursues a successful career instead. Decades later, the old general enjoys a sumptuous feast in the simple home of Martina and her sister, prepared by the Parisian Babette. He raises a glass and speaks of redemption despite lost dreams and the setbacks of his own life:

> There comes a time when our eyes are opened and we come to
> realize that mercy is infinite…. Mercy imposes no conditions.
> And lo! Everything we have chosen has been granted to us.
> And everything we rejected has also been granted. Yes, we even
> get back what we rejected.

I trust that this is true, not only for the dreams we have "rejected" but also the ones that have been lost or defeated along the way.

I trust that it is true even on a grand scale: As a Christian, I believe in a God whose dream appeared defeated by Jesus' death on a cross, but whose Dream shines through in resurrection. God's dreams for each person may *appear* defeated by illness, loss, and death—but they are all part of the dream of abundant and eternal life. That cosmic redemption renews my faith in the redemption General Lowenhielm articulates. It encourages me to join my farming friends in the kind of durable, long-haul hope that survives setbacks of all kinds.

Evidence of healing

This hope is a sign of love, which survives, often in spite of ourselves. This is a remarkable paradox of human life: we are simultaneously fragile and incredibly resilient. We have enormous potential for healing when Love comes in and creates a new beginning, again and again. There is no guarantee that we won't be hurt along the way, but what happens after the hurt can be powerful evidence of love. On our bodies, minds, and hearts, we get to keep the scars to remind us of this evidence.

Fortunately, my scars are on my face where I can see them every day— "fortunately" because I greatly need daily reminders of this healing. They come from a car accident when I was eleven. On the way home from a church event, a pickup truck ran a red light and smashed into the side of our tiny Chevette. As we spun around the intersection, my friend and I in the backseat crashed our heads together. She had seen the truck coming and ducked, so the hard top of her head crushed the right side of my face and broke several bones. No one else was injured.

It's easy to find evidence of love here and to tell the story of the time that followed as a love story. Through the recovery time and the surgery to repair my face, people did what they so often do in trying times: they surrounded my family with support, cards, and food. As an eleven-year-old, I had never seen such a thing before, and it was a revelation. My family, distant from relatives, had always been self-sufficient. We were usually the ones who helped, not the ones who received help. So I had no idea, for example, that a pastor would actually come to visit *me* in the hospital. (He read me Psalm 121. I felt cared for and important.) Those remarkable times of healing are easy to forget as time goes on, so I am fortunate to have the evidence right where I can see it.

When we tell the love story of our journey amid a life that offers no guarantees, it is essential that we include evidence that some areas have healed and that we have survived to continue on our journey another day. Paul writes,

> We also boast in our sufferings, knowing that suffering pro-
> duces endurance, and endurance produces character, and char-
> acter produces hope, and hope does not disappoint us, because
> God's love has been poured into our hearts through the Holy
> Spirit that has been given to us (Rom. 5.3–5).

It is tempting to "boast in our sufferings" as evidence that we have been damaged beyond repair. But we have another choice: we can also tell of healing, survival, and connection. Of course, no one can dictate that interpretation for someone else. Suffering is not automatically re-demptive. But there seems to be an intuitive connection between scars and evidence of God's healing presence. In confirmation class with mid-dle-school students one evening, we were studying the story of Jesus appearing to the disciples on the road to Emmaus after his resurrection (Luke 24:13–35). I asked the kids to draw a "life map" and mark out places where they had met Jesus along the road. Discussing the maps later, not many told stories of times when everything worked out perfectly. Instead, many told stories of scars on their bodies and hearts—an accident, the death of a loved one, an illness, a difficult move. We can and often do tell those stories as love stories—evidence of God's power at work and of our resilience, which responds to that powerful love.

> *Clue:* Do you or does someone you know frequently "boast of hardship," telling "ain't it awful" stories of victimhood or martyrdom? What is gained from such stories? What might happen if you told those stories as love stories instead?

Love endures

In the face of a life of no guarantees, it's easy to wonder what could possibly last through life's ups and downs. My students often wondered this about the next step down the road. Did they have the patience and endurance to hang in there with friendships, a significant relationship, perhaps eventually marriage and parenthood? Did they have the willpower to persevere with graduate school and support themselves over the long haul? Did they have a passion deep enough to sustain them in a career over time—would their life's work, if and when they find it, really last a lifetime? Would they be able to accomplish, learn, craft, or beget something in their lifetime that would endure? There are no guarantees about any of these, and the best discernment is no insurance against the unexpected.

It's often said that in a vocation, "What gets you into it isn't what keeps you in it." In other words, whatever inspiration or passion compels you to enter it, that usually passes. And then, if the vocation is to endure, something else must emerge that helps you stay there. That's true of work, marriage, friendships, and community. In John 15, Jesus talks about what endures and *how* to endure. The chapter culminates in the promise that for one who follows Jesus, his or her life will "bear fruit,

fruit that will last." It sounds like the answer to sustaining a vocation: To do that, the text says, one must "remain" or "abide" in Jesus and his love.[5] One must stay close to God's dream and God's passionate love for us.

It sounds simple, but not when I consider doing this *every single day*. So many things pull me out of Jesus' love—resentments, fears, and busyness, to name just a few. I have my moments of good spiritual discipline—such as prayer, Scripture reading, kindness to others—but "momentary discipline" is an oxymoron. If it were up to us to abide in Jesus, we would fail completely. No wonder we cannot sustain any vocation on our own.

Fortunately, it's not up to us. In that same chapter of John, Jesus talks about laying down one's life: "No one has greater love than this, to lay down one's life for one's friends" (v. 13). Typical. Every time I think I'm required to hold on tightly, keep my nose to the grindstone, grit my teeth, and *endure*, Jesus comes back and says it's really not about that: It's about letting go. Not only that, but Jesus has already done that for us. That Greek word for "laying down" is *tithēmi* again, "to put." It shows up again several verses later: "You did not choose me, but I chose you and *appointed* you to go and bear fruit." Apparently, Jesus has already laid us down. He has put us in the places where we are invited to surrender our very lives, and give what we have to offer.

Does that mean Christians never change jobs or get divorced? Not at all. In fact, it reminds us again that there is no guarantee that those externals in our lives will last. What lasts is the relationship with God through Christ—which Jesus describes in John 15 as "friendship" (vv. 14–15). Friendship with Christ is what lasts not because we hold on to him but because in laying down *his* life, he holds on to us. Our vocations are places where that friendship gets lived out—the roles may change, but the friendship endures.

This radical notion of surrender leads to a whole different understanding of what those externals in our lives—our vocations as parents, workers, spouses, students, and so on—really mean. What we appear to lose in surrender, we receive back in Jesus' friendship. And then, in the life of discipleship, God gives the other things back to us as gifts, which show up in our multiple vocations. When you keep following Jesus, when you keep putting one foot in front of the other on the path he lays out before you, when you stay focused on that one thing, other things eventually fall into place—work, relationships, recreation. They become gifts that can bring us closer to God and form us into the people God made us.

God's love and Christ's friendship last. They endure through all our endings and beginnings, our changes and even our wounds. Saint Ignatius calls this the "First Principle and Foundation": through all our callings and circumstances, God draws us closer. "The goal of our life is to live with God forever.... All the things in this world are gifts of God, presented to us so that we can know God more easily and make a return of love more readily."

God gives the gifts; *our* part is letting go of our need for guarantees and our desire to "endure" on our own. "As a result, we appreciate and use all these gifts of God insofar as they help us develop as loving persons. But if any of these gifts becomes the center of our lives, they displace God and so hinder our growth toward our goal." Our hope of guarantees can cause us to cling to clues, hoping they are treasure. But when God calls us back to the big Dream, sometimes we have to let go of the small-d dreams. "Our only desire and our one choice should be this: I want and I choose what better leads to God's deepening life in me."[6]

'All the way to heaven is heaven'

"God's deepening life in me": that's a much different kind of "happily ever after." In this kind, we don't have to wait till "ever after" to live happily. After all, in the incarnation, God committed to our journeys in *this* life.

A few months after I began work at Santa Clara University, I was preparing to lead my very first vocation retreat with students. The day before the retreat, I received a phone call from a friend of my friend Ingrid. He told me Ingrid had died suddenly at home the day before; no one knew how.

I was stunned and considered canceling the retreat, but somehow the retreat seemed the best way to honor her. Ingrid and I had shared an apartment in our mid-twenties. It was a time of vocational turmoil for both of us as we discerned jobs and relationships. Our apartment and our later conversations had been places of wrestling with questions and wondering where we would "end up." It had never occurred to me—or to her, I imagine—that an "ending" would come so quickly, with so much treasure undiscovered.

When she died, Ingrid had still been searching in her career, and she had married just the year before. From my perspective, at least, she seemed very much in the middle of her journey. So that was my question for the retreat: because Ingrid's treasure hunt had been curtailed after only thirty years, did it mean she had failed to find her vocation? That answer was unthinkable to me. She had lived with so much love, and with an integrity to her search that I longed to have in my own life. I thought of Saint Catherine of Siena, who declared, in the face of anxious longing and seeking: "All the way to heaven is heaven." Ingrid's life showed me that it's also true that "all the way to vocation is vocation." The search is paramount, not the finding. The search is even the treasure, because that is where God finds us in our capacity to love and to seek, in our experiences of healing, and in an amazing Dream. The search is where we find ourselves.

From Ingrid's life, I came to understand that the search is also bigger than this lifetime. God's dream does not end; God's commitment to our human journeys goes on. I believe that's why, in becoming human, Jesus had to continue his own journey to the grave and beyond—so he could accompany us when our journey takes *us* there. That's how passionately God loves us. It's true, there are no guarantees. As Ingrid taught me, there's not even a guarantee that any of us will have enough time in this life to continue searching until something "turns out." But paradoxically she also gave me a way to become more peaceful with my own sense of being unfinished, with so much still undiscovered.

Many things can cast out fear and anxiety and help you trust the journey:

- your ability to seek and to love
- the existence of a big dream, whether you can name it or not
- the experience of healing
- the presence of love,which suffuses and transcends human life.

When we find these things along the way, we are not far from the kingdom of God. That, in fact, is Jesus' response to the anxiety of his disciples: Seek God's kingdom, and the things you need will be given to you as well.

No, there are no guarantees. But there are hopes—so many hopes for how we will receive and give and love along the way. Hope is so much sturdier than guarantees. Guarantees fall apart if they're not carefully protected, but hope can carry its own weight. You can live with hope, and it can handle everyday use. Hope travels well.

Our journey teaches us this hope, or rather forms it in us. Hope that God's love really is eternal. Hope that we can live happily and let God, in God's infinite possibility, take care of the ever after. Hope that with the skills we learn on our search for treasure, we will one day love God, the world, and ourselves as passionately as we are loved.

Further exploration

On your life as a love story:

- *The Awakened Heart: Opening Yourself to the Love You Need,* by Gerald G. May, is a personal and wise guide to spiritual life and love (San Francisco: HarperSanFrancisco, 1991).
- In his hopeful book *The Inner Voice of Love: A Journey Through Anguish to Freedom,* Henri J. M. Nouwen shares thoughts from his personal struggle and offers evidence of healing through love, God, and community. (Image Books, 1999).
- Gloria Gaynor's classic song, "I Will Survive," reminds us that even after heartbreak, "knowing how to love" is the essence of survival (*I Will Survive: The Anthology,* Universal Motown Records, 1998).
- Dan B. Allender's book, *To Be Told: God Invites You to Coauthor Your Future,* includes examples and questions for telling your own story and noticing "the themes that God has written there" (Colorado Springs: WaterBrook Press, 2005).

On faith in a big enough dream:

- "Hold It Up to the Light," a song by David Wilcox, captures both the confidence and the anxiety of the journey toward one's dreams (*Big Horizon,* A&M Records, 1994).
- Sharon Daloz Parks' *Big Questions, Worthy Dreams* is not written for a young-adult audience but rather for older adults invested in what the subtitle says: *Mentoring Young Adults in Their Search for Meaning, Purpose, and Faith.* However, I read it as a young-adult pastor and appreciated the way young adults' stories and her use of developmental theories helped me understand my own development better (San Francisco: Jossey-Bass, 2000).

Epilogue

The best way to help me find my story is to tell me your story.
—Ernest Kurtz and Katherine Ketcham[1]

IN THE FIVE YEARS since I began writing this book, my journey has taken several twists and turns I couldn't have seen coming. Not necessarily in this order: I have moved three times; became divorced from my husband; left one job, and after six months of waiting, started another; adopted a second cat; and bought my first home. I have performed at least ten funerals and ten weddings and preached countless sermons. Along with significant losses, the journey has overflowed with abundant grace. A large part of that grace came through the call to write this book and to talk with others, privately and publicly, about the journey of vocation discernment. It's very difficult to wallow in self-pity for one's own trials and tribulations when you have to keep talking about God's abundant grace, and when people keep sharing with you the difficult twists and turns of *their* journeys as well as the ways they've experienced grace and beauty.

The process of writing this book has provided me a shelter from life's storms. This was the kind of shelter I had been looking for in my parents' spare bedroom, but I should have known that this kind of shelter comes internally more than externally. I should have known because I learned it years ago from a woman named Rebecca Cox Jackson, a woman who lived in mid-nineteenth century Philadelphia. I encountered her in my early twenties, when her autobiography, *Gifts of Power*,[2] became the subject of my senior thesis in college.

Jackson had a remarkable journey. She discerned her way into and out of religious communities more times than most modern adults I knew. Jackson began her story as a married woman rooted in the African Methodist Episcopal Church. By the end, she had founded a Shaker community unlike any other, with both black and white members and located in the middle of the city. In between, she had been called to celibacy, joined the Holiness movement, became an itinerant preacher, explored Spiritualism, and joined, left, and rejoined the Shakers. Long before the saying, "Take what you like and leave the rest," Jackson took helpful pieces of tradition and created something brand new out of them. In her autobiography, she describes a dream that illustrates and names her faith-building work. Overlooking a field full of ruined buildings, she saw people moving among the ruins picking up bricks, ready to build something new. Her life was a long journey picking up the bricks of various traditions on how God works, but all the while she was building and rebuilding a new theological house where she could find shelter.

We all need a theology and ways of living it which can withstand the storms of life. If you've been exploring the clues in this book, you've been working on understanding how you experience and believe God to be at work in your life and journey. I hope you'll use those bricks to build a shelter from the current or future storms in your life. And I hope you'll share those bricks with someone else, too. No one can do this journey for us, but none of us does it alone. As we learn from the journey, as we seek our callings and encounter God and find ourselves, over and over, we are building and rebuilding shelter for ourselves. Eventually, we find ourselves dwelling within the journey, where we are both at home *and* on the way.

The shelter we find and make is not for ourselves alone. At times of transition or trouble, we need our own stories, but we need others', too.

"Remember only this one thing, the stories people tell have a way of taking care of them. If stories come to you, care for them. And learn to give them away when they are needed. Sometimes a person needs a story—more than food to stay alive."[3] To find this community and the stories you need, offer them.

Someone needs your story—perhaps because your story is different, or perhaps because it is the same. There is an old fable of a man who travels an entire kingdom, repeatedly telling a story that he had been given, until one of his listeners recognizes it as his own story. With relief and joy, he explains that he had been told, "When someone tells you your own story, you will know you have been redeemed."[4]

Through mutual storytelling, we find the strength to hold on to what is good and life-giving and let go of what was painful and death-dealing—we too learn to "take what we like and leave the rest." Of the bricks we've discovered or have been given, we choose which ones can build a strong shelter. Others, we release. Our journeys teach us trust, and they can teach us forgiveness, too. At some point, we forgive our lives for how they are turning out: the twists and turns we did not choose, the clues we thought were "the one," the scars of body and soul we have acquired along the way. Like redemption, forgiveness often comes when we see how our journey can be helpful to someone else.

Young adults have taught me that for each of us, our own journey is the greatest gift we have to offer, as we share what we have come to love along the way. Once when I was shaking my head at something wonderful I had just noticed that God was doing in my life, I wondered if everyone was in on this mysterious grace. Could *everyone* see the new creation, and was it only me who was slow to figure out that it was just steps away? I asked God, "Do they know how amazing life is?" God didn't say yes or no—just said, "Tell them." So I've done my best to do that—to share stories of witnessing God's grace, abundance, beauty, and companionship, in the hope that they will remind you of your own stories.

Of course, in the scheme of things, it's not much—it's about as significant as a tiny mustard seed in the midst of a much larger field of conversation. But it's the mustard seed I've been given, and I'm grateful for it. And so at this point on my journey, as I have done at many other junctures, I offer a prayer written by Dag Hammarskjöld:[5]

"For all that has been—thanks! For all that shall be—yes!"

Acknowledgements

THIS BOOK BEGAN WITH A STORY OF FEELING ALONE, but it ends with community and with gratitude for all those who have been revealed as "good company" along the way. I'm especially grateful to those who have come to look for me and who have provided clues, company along the way, and the courage to keep following the clues no matter where they led. I hope the book itself expresses my deep gratitude.

So many people have provided good company to me that it's impossible to mention them all. However, I want to acknowledge by name some who also provided good company for this book. Many people and organizations "heard me into speech" by inviting me to speak on these topics, and parts of the book appeared first in those forms. A more secular version of Chapter 1 was first a keynote address to a high school leadership conference. Many times I have thanked Jake Fuller for the invitation to speak, which led to the crystallizing of the treasure hunt metaphor over lunch one day in the Santa Clara University cafeteria. Chapter 7 grew from a retreat for spouses of clergy in the Sierra Pacific Synod of the Lutheran Church (ELCA). Parts of the Invitation and Chapter 9 came from an address to the Western Mission Network of ELCA institutions and a retreat with the Tri-Ota region of the Lutheran Student Movement. Scattered throughout the book are sermons addressed to a variety of congregations—most significantly, to two congregations who have shaped, supported, and challenged me by calling me to be their pastor: Prince of Peace Lutheran Church in Saratoga, California, and Lutheran Church of the Good Shepherd in Reno, Nevada.

I'm grateful to people I have encountered in those congregations and in other communities of discernment over the years—sometimes only in brief kairos moments—who have shared their stories with me. Young-adult groups at the two congregations I have served have helped shape this book, and so has the annual women's retreat of Lutheran Church of the Good Shepherd.

Parts of the book began in written form elsewhere. Some of Chapter 5 emerged from papers at Pacific Lutheran Theological Seminary while I was working toward my Master of Divinity degree; I'm grateful for that education which really did "draw out" the person and pastor I am still in the process of becoming. Other parts of the book first appeared in a weekly column on United Press International's Religion and Spirituality Forum in 2006 and 2007 (www.religionandspirituality.com). I am grateful for that forum, where the community and the weekly deadline helped this book get written.

I appreciate the contributions of Lilly Endowment Inc. to so many valuable projects related to vocation, including Programs for the Theological Exploration of Vocation. This book is an indirect result of such contributions, since it was profoundly shaped by my experience on the Lilly-funded project at Santa Clara University known as DISCOVER (Developing and Inspiring Scholarly Communities Oriented toward Vocational Engagement and Reflection, www.scu.edu/discover.) In one of those clues that dramatically changes the direction of a journey, Martha E. Stortz (or Marty) first encouraged me to apply for the position and continued to be a significant conversation partner, friend, and mentor throughout my time at Santa Clara.

It's impossible to name all the significant conversation partners at

Santa Clara, but my direct colleagues on the DISCOVER project deserve special mention for their intelligent and whole-hearted leadership and inspirational vision: Chris Boscia, Michael Colyer, Elizabeth Eilers Sullivan, Elizabeth Thompson, Christie Heit, Mark Ravizza, S.J., Dennis Moberg, and especially the late Bill Spohn, the original project director. Beth Eilers and I enjoyed a creative partnership in developing a five-week "discernment training" curriculum for students, where she introduced me to contemplative listening, among other helpful ideas and practices. I also learned much by writing an article with Elizabeth Thompson, "Letting Your Life Speak," and that thought process infuses parts of the Invitation and some of Chapter 7. Throughout the book, some of the resources for "Further Exploration" were first brought to my attention by such resourceful colleagues. For asking big questions, dreaming worthy dreams, and wrestling with the mysteries of vocation, no one could ask for more creative and compassionate colleagues.

Along with DISCOVER, the Santa Clara Campus Ministry staff, Residence Life staff, Residential Learning Communities leaders, Resident Ministers, the Religious Studies department, and the student leaders of Core Christian Fellowship provided a supportive home for me and my work. I appreciate Mario Prietto, S.J., and others who made this born-and-bred Lutheran feel at home among Jesuits. I'm especially grateful to Paul Crowley, S.J., who mentored me in the Ignatian tradition and spiritual direction and witnessed this book emerging in our conversations. Various departments and student organizations at Santa Clara gave me the honor of leading retreats for their groups, and the effects on the book of those days spent in conversation are too numerous to mention.

Many thanks to those who read part or all of the book, provided helpful feedback, and when I was tempted to take the book back into hiding, encouraged me to let it see the light of day: Sylvia Seymour, Kathleen McDavid, Shaun O'Reilly, Ginny McBride, Carl Wilfrid, Deanna Gaunt, Mary Lou Petitjean, Carol Jacobson, and Marty Stortz. Carolyn Foster's coaching and retreats have nourished my soul and helped to identify some "Further Exploration" resources.

In the publishing process, this book found some very good friends with the gift of helping something become what it is trying to be. Naomi Lucks and Teresa Castle were attentive and encouraging editors. Bob Blesse not only designed the cover and the book, but he and Victoria Davies also offered essential and supportive advice along the way.

No one can give away what they have not first received. I have received so much from so many, and everything good in this book can be attributed to someone who first gave it to me. However, from those "bricks" of ideas and experiences I have created my own house, so any errors or omissions are fully my responsibility.

Finally, I need to acknowledge the three people who were always part of the excitement on Christmas morning when I discovered my first clue in the bottom of my stocking. My sister, Amy Gonsalves, and I have sometimes followed very different sets of clues in life as well as in Christmas presents, but I have always learned much from her journey. My parents, Jim and Mary Schlatter, have provided many clues and much good company along the way, and they have been indispensable to this book, too. Throughout my journey I have been a typical young adult periodically "boomeranging" back under their roof, and much of this book was written in their spare bedroom. They have lovingly provided not only physical shelter but also a remarkable faith in the journey. More than thirty years after the first Christmas treasure hunt, they are still convinced, along with me, that there is a treasure around here somewhere and whatever else it may be, it will be a gift.

Chapter Notes

Invitation

[1] Walter Brueggemann, *Texts Under Negotiation: The Bible and Postmodern Imagination* (Minneapolis: Augsburg Fortress, 1993), 19–21. He writes, "My topic is a more modest one: *funding* postmodern imagination. It is not, in my judgment, the work of the church (or of the preacher) to construct a full alternative world. ... Rather, the task is to *fund*—to provide the pieces, materials, and resources out of which a new world can be imagined."

[2] Marion Woodman, *Addiction to Perfection: The Still Unravished Bride* (Toronto: Inner City Books, 1982), 129.

Chapter 1

[1] *Indiana Jones and the Last Crusade* (Lucasfilm, 1989).

[2] Quoted in Gregg Levoy, *Callings: Finding and Following an Authentic Life* (New York: Three Rivers Press, 1997), 261.

[3] For example, see Martin Luther on the theology of the cross in his "Heidelberg Disputation," especially nos. 20-21. In *Martin Luther's Basic Theological Writing,* ed. Timothy F. Lull (Minneapolis: Fortress Press, 1989), 43–44.

[4] From a video series called "Intersections—Three Key Questions." For Intersections, a discernment project at Boston College, Michael Himes narrated three brief videos, one on each question. You can find them at www.food4thought.tv.

[5] Frederick Buechner, *Wishful Thinking: A Seeker's ABC* (San Francisco: Harper, 1992), 119.

[6] For example, see Roger Ferlo, *Sensing God: Reading Scripture with All Our Senses* (Cambridge, Mass.: Cowley Publications, 2002).

[7] Sharon D. Welch, *A Feminist Ethic of Risk* (Minneapolis: Fortress Press, 2000).

[8] Anne Lamott, *Traveling Mercies: Some Thoughts on Faith* (New York: Anchor Books, 1999), 3.

[9]Luther writes this to his friend and colleague Philip Melanchthon, August 1, 1521. *Luther's Works,* American edition (St. Louis and Philadelphia: Concordia and Fortress Press, 1958–1986), v. 48, pp. 281-82.

Chapter 2

[1]Benedicta Ward, S.L.G., trans., Poemen 63, in *The Sayings of the Desert Fathers* (London and Oxford: Mowbray, 1981), 175.
[2]*The Legend of Bagger Vance* (Dreamworks, 2000).
[3]Nelle Morton, *The Journey Is Home* (Boston: Beacon Press, 1985), 55–56.
[4]*Dead Poets Society* (Touchstone Pictures, 1989).

Chapter 3

[1]Charles Du Bos, *Approximations, 1922-1937.*
[2]P.D. Eastman, *Are You My Mother?* (New York: Random House, 1960).
[3]I first found this quoted in Ernest Kurtz and Katherine Ketcham, *The Spirituality of Imperfection: Storytelling and the Search for Meaning* (New York: Bantam Books, 1992), 2. It comes from Martin Buber, *Tales of the Hasidim: The Early Masters* (New York: Schocken Books, 1975), 251.
[4]In 2004, the United Church of Christ denomination developed its "God is still speaking" advertising campaign using a comma as its symbol, with reference to Allen's quote.
[5]Matthew 10:39 and 16:25, Mark 8:35, Luke 9:24 and 17:33, and John 12:25.
[6]Dietrich Bonhoeffer, *The Cost of Discipleship* (New York: Touchstone, 1995).
[7]I later heard a similar comment in an episode of "Sex and the City," so that may have been my friend's source.

Chapter 4

[1]André Gide, *The Counterfeiters,* trans. Dorothy Bussy (New York: Alfred A. Knopf, 1949), 326.

[2]Paul Tillich, *The Courage to Be* (New Haven and London: Yale University Press, 1980), 190.

[3]Parker J. Palmer, *Let Your Life Speak: Listening for the Voice of Vocation* (San Francisco: Jossey-Bass, 2000), 37-55.

[4]Fred Luskin, *Forgive for Good: A Proven Prescription for Health and Happiness*, (San Francisco: HarperSanFrancisco, 2002).

[5]Similar to other folkloric stories that capture an essence of the human condition, the "two wolves" story shows up in so many forms and places that it is difficult to pinpoint one source. Many attribute it to a Native American tradition. You can find various references for the story at http://www.story-lovers.com/listswolfifeedstory.html.

[6]Thomas Merton, *Thoughts in Solitude* (New York: Farrar, Straus, and Giroux, 1958).

Chapter 5

[1]Apparently this sentiment wasn't unique in my own relation to God. After praying this sentence all year—"God, couldn't you have done whatever you're doing *some other way*?"—I later found I had read it long before in *Martin Luther's Christmas Book*. There, Luther reflects on the incarnation and birth of Jesus and asks, "Could not God have saved the world some other way?" (Ed. Roland H. Bainton [Minneapolis: Augsburg Fortress, 1997], 40.)

[2]Barbara Kingsolver, *Prodigal Summer* (New York: HarperCollins, 2000).

[3]Thanks to Carrie Grev for this helpful and hopeful phrase.

[4]Palmer, 10–12.

[5]I attended Le Collège Cevenol in the summer of 1989, the same year Pierre Sauvage produced the film and well before the Internet made this information widely available. President Barack Obama referred to Le Chambon's story in his Holocaust Remembrance address on April 23, 2009 (http://www.whitehouse.gov/the_press_office/Remarks-by-the-President-at-the-Holocaust-Days-of-Remembrance-Ceremony/).

[6]*Weapons of the Spirit* (Sauvage Productions, 1989).

[7] Philip Hallie, *Lest Innocent Blood Be Shed: The Story of the Village of Le Chambon and How Goodness Happened There* (New York: Harper & Row, 1979).

[8] Palmer, 88-89.

[9] Athanasius of Alexandria, in *The Incarnation of the Word of God*, Refutation of the Gentiles, no. 54.

[10] In *Peripheral Visions: Learning Along the Way*, Mary Catherine Bateson talks about her journey as a spiral (New York: HarperCollins, 1994). *Walking a Literary Labyrinth: A Spirituality of Reading*, by Nancy M. Malone, may have been the first place I encountered a labyrinth pattern for a spiritual journey (New York: Riverhead Books, 2003).

[11] I am grateful to David Eppelsheimer for this meaningful and memorable image.

Chapter 6

[1] *Occasional Services*, a Companion to the Lutheran Book of Worship (Minneapolis: Augsburg Publishing House, and Philadelphia: Board of Publication, Lutheran Church in America, 1982), 194 and others.

[2] Oriah Mountain Dreamer, *The Call: Discovering Why You Are Here* (San Francisco: HarperSanFrancisco, 2003), 180–181.

[3] *The Secret Garden* (American Zoetrope, 1993).

[4] The questions were inspired by Russell B. Connors, Jr. and Patrick T. McCormick, *Character, Choices, and Community: The Three Faces of Christian Ethics* (Mahwah, NJ: Paulist Press, 1998).

[5] *Shadowlands* (Price Entertainment, 1993).

[6] Annie Dillard, "An Expedition to the Pole," in *Teaching a Stone to Talk: Expeditions and Encounters* (New York: Harper & Row, 1982), 31.

[7] "Take Our Bread," written by Joe Wise. Here the words have been adapted, perhaps by the church where I learned the song. The original words apparently were, "Poor though we are, we have brought ourselves to you." Found in the collection *Gonna Sing, My Lord* (GIA Publications, 1967).

Chapter 7

[1] Henri J. M. Nouwen, *Reaching Out: The Three Movements of the Spiritual Life* (New York: Doubleday, 1986), 53.
[2] Max Weber, *From Max Weber: Essays in Sociology*, ed. and trans. H. H. Gerth and C. Wright Mills (New York: Oxford University Press, 1946), 325.
[3] Robin McKenzie and Craig Kubey, *7 Steps to a Pain-Free Life* (New York: Penguin, 2000); Creflo A. Dollar, *8 Steps to Create the Life You Want* (New York: Hachette Book Group, 2008); and Suze Orman, *The 9 Steps to Financial Freedom* (New York: Three Rivers Press, 1997).
[4] Dietrich Bonhoeffer, *Life Together: The Classic Exploration of Faith in Community*, trans. John W. Doberstein (San Francisco: HarperSanFrancisco, 1954), 77, *original emphasis*.

Chapter 8

[1] Henri J.M. Nouwen, *Lifesigns: Intimacy, Fecundity, and Ecstasy in Christian Perspective* (New York: Doubleday, 1989), 29.
[2] The concept of "path vs. place" is not original to me; it was brought to my attention by Martha Stortz.
[3] Kathleen Norris, *Amazing Grace: A Vocabulary of Faith* (New York: Riverhead Books, 1998), 56.
[4] Roberta Bondi, *To Love as God Loves* (Philadelphia: Fortress Press, 1987), 60–61.
[5] Himes video, "Intersections—Three Key Questions," Part 3 of 3, "Does Anyone Need You To Do It?"
[6] J. Ruth Gendler, *Notes on the Need for Beauty: An Intimate Look at an Essential Quality* (New York: Marlowe & Co., 2007), 86.
[7] Marianne Williamson, *A Return to Love* (New York: HarperPerennial, 1993), 190–191.
[8] Erik Erikson, *Identity and the Life Cycle* (New York: Norton, 1980), 100–103, 129.
[9] Martha Beck, *Finding Your Own North Star: Claiming the Life You Were Meant to Live* (New York: Three Rivers Press, 2001), 60-75.

Chapter 9

[1]Paulo Coelho, *The Alchemist: A Fable about Following Your Dreams,* trans. Alan R. Clarke (San Francisco: HarperSanFrancisco, 1993), 122.
[2]May Sarton, "Now I Become Myself," in *Collected Poems, 1930–1973* (New York: Norton, 1974), 156. Quoted in Palmer, 9.
[3]Douglas J. Schuurman, *Vocation: Discerning Our Callings in Life* (Grand Rapids, MI: William B. Eerdmans Publishing Co., 2004), 119.
[4]This saying is most frequently attributed to Saint Augustine of Hippo or Saint Ignatius of Loyola.
[5]Parker J. Palmer, *To Know as We Are Known: Education as a Spiritual Journey* (San Francisco: HarperSanFrancisco, 1993), 43.
[6]*August Rush* (Warner Bros. Pictures, 2007).
[7]Michael Harter, S.J., ed., *Hearts on Fire: Praying with Jesuits* (Chicago: Loyola Press, 2004), 8.
[8]Shel Silverstein, *The Missing Piece* (New York: HarperCollins, 1976).

Chapter 10

[1]Dag Hammarskjöld, *Markings,* trans. Leif Sjöberg and W. H. Auden (New York: Alfred A. Knopf, 1964), 81.
[2]Gerald G. May, *The Awakened Heart: Opening Yourself to the Love You Need* (San Francisco: HarperSanFrancisco, 1991), 21.
[3]Sharon Daloz Parks, *Big Questions, Worthy Dreams: Mentoring Young Adults in Their Search for Meaning, Purpose, and Faith* (San Francisco: Jossey-Bass, 2000), 146.
[4]*Babette's Feast* (Panorama Film A/S, 1989).
[5]To follow the Greek word *meno* (abide, stay, remain, dwell) through John's gospel is to discover the meaning of incarnation, God-become-flesh: the enduring possibility for dwelling with God. In addition to multiple instances in John 15, see John 1:39, 4:40, 6:56, 8:35, and 14:16–17.
[6]Paraphrase by David L. Fleming, S.J., in Harter, ed., *Hearts on Fire,* 7-8 (http://issuu.com/loyolapress/docs/hearts_on_fire.)